Sophie Grigson's
Travels à la Carte

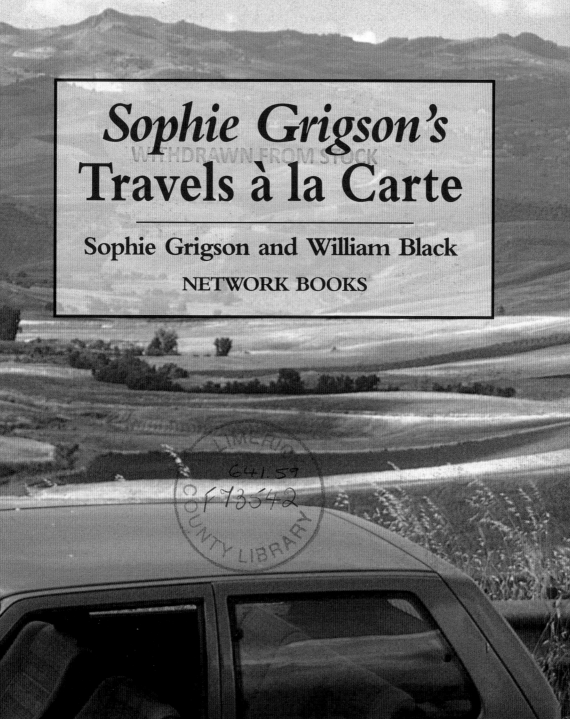

Sophie Grigson's Travels à la Carte

Sophie Grigson and William Black

NETWORK BOOKS

For Florence

Network Books is an imprint of BBC Books,
a division of BBC Enterprises Limited
Woodlands, 80 Wood Lane, London W 12 0TT

First published 1994

ISBN 0 563 37017 3

Designed by Tim Higgins

Set in Monotype Bembo and Photina by Selwood Systems, Midsomer Norton
Printed and bound in Great Britain by Butler & Tanner Ltd, Frome
Colour separations by Radstock Reproductions, Midsomer Norton
Jacket printed by Lawrence Allen Ltd, Weston-super-Mare

Picture Credits

Food photography by Jess Koppel
Styling by Roisin Nield
Home Economist: Lyn Rutherford

All other photos by Cassie Farrell/Scorer Associates
except page 10 by J. Allan Cash

Step-by-step illustrations by Kate Simunek

PREVIOUS PAGES
A dispute about directions in Sicily.

Contents

Acknowledgements

As we travelled around Europe, we were struck by the endless generosity of the people we met. This book would not exist without the help of all those people in Spain, Portugal, Italy, France, Switzerland, Norway, Hungary and Turkey who gave us a glimpse of their lives and food. Though there are too many to name them all, we'd particularly like to thank Laura Reis, the Lerchi family, Marcus, Sarolta Schutz, Paulette and Jean-Pierre Picot, the Fouteau family, Ayhan, Alicia Rios, and Felisa and Anastasio Zamorano.

Credit for the original idea belongs to Mischa Scorer, who together with Cassie Farrell directed the television series. Mischa's suggestion that William and I should co-present ensured that we were able to spend more time together, which was a marvellous bonus. Mischa and Sue Shephard of Channel 4 were remarkably calm when, a week before the beginning of filming, I broke the news that I was pregnant. Many thanks to them for their unwavering confidence in us, despite my increasing girth.

Paul and David Otter and Jane Barnett were endlessly supportive, kept us laughing throughout and tactfully steered us in the right direction. Cassie Farrell and Harriet Batten-Foster proved to be tireless dogged researchers, leaving no stone unturned, and making our job much easier.

Heather Holden-Brown, Frank Phillips and Deborah Taylor of Network Books have, yet again, been paragons of patience. The beautiful food photography comes from my favourite photographic trio: Jess Koppel on camera, Lyn Rutherford at the stove and Roisin Nield on pots and dishes.

William wishes to extend special thanks to all at Cutty Catering who long-sufferingly put up with his frequent absences without batting an eyelid. On the home front, three assistants – Margaret Brooker, Deborah Greatrex and Annabel Hartog – have provided invaluable help, endlessly testing recipes, keeping me cheerful and positive, organizing my papers, my life and my kitchen cupboards. Grace Mukasa has been more patient than I deserve, happily feeding the cats and working her way around the piles of debris and half-unpacked suitcases that took over the house.

OPPOSITE
Sophie and William lunch with friends in Gascony.

Introduction

―――――――

This book is a record of eight journeys we made in 1993. When I look back over the year, I realize how exceedingly lucky we've been. Work has provided us with an excuse to indulge in what is probably our favourite pastime – travelling, with plenty of eating on the side – to an almost absurd extent.

Eight journeys, eight different countries and eight very different cuisines. We confined ourselves to Europe, though in the widest continental sense, which meant that we could squeeze in Norway, Hungary and Istanbul. We had a wonderful time: we ate a lot, we learnt a lot and, most enjoyable of all, we met many generous people, happy to share their time, their expertise and their enthusiasm. The Christmas card list has almost doubled in size.

An interest in food is a wonderful door-opener when you travel. Even the mildest expression of curiosity about local cooking or produce can lead to invitations to come and see, to explore, to discover not just culinary traditions, but the wider culture of an area too. Food is often – no, is usually the pivot around which society has been built. A shared morning in the kitchen or out in the fields and orchards may lay the foundation for a much more extensive education, not to mention an

unexpected friendship. With recipes come nuggets of juicy information – old superstitions, long-held habits, small daily rituals, farming lore – all those things that contribute to the daily life of a community.

In the chapters that follow I've made no attempt to be comprehensive about the cuisine of any one country – how can you sum up endless regional variations in a few short pages? – nor have I been particularly analytical. No, what there is here is definitely anecdotal and distinctly personal, a series of impressions, that will, I hope, give a taste of the places we visited, both in the metaphorical and, when you try the recipes, literal sense.

In each chapter William has contributed a piece on some area of food production or industry that he found particularly interesting. The observant will notice that fish feature strongly. This is not surprising: there is nothing in the world that interests him more than fish! He works with them, he reads about them, he talks about them, and he eats them with unabandoned relish. Though he suffered brief deprivations in the land-locked areas of France, Switzerland, Spain and Hungary that we visited, Portugal and Norway proved to be veritable paradises.

Fish or no fish, trying to recreate foreign dishes back on home territory inevitably means a certain degree of compromise. Where this or that ingredient is not available, or is different in flavour, or, worse still, is vastly inferior, I've had to adapt and tweak to get something close to the original. On the whole, though I say it myself, I've done a pretty good job of it, and where I failed miserably the recipe ended up rejected and in the bin. On pages 210–214 I've given further details of special ingredients and suggestions for substitutes if necessary.

There is, in any case, no such thing as a definitive recipe for a traditional dish. At least, it is very rare indeed. Every cook who carries forward the methods she inherited from her mother, her grandmother, her great-grandmother, is likely to have her own particular quirks and secrets, developed over the years. What emerges from the oven may be similar to what her equally knowledgeable neighbour sets on the table, but it will never be the same. That is the nature, the joy of those dishes that have been cherished and repeated time and again, through generation after generation, improved, updated, personalized, simplified or embellished.

Though each region, each country has fed us in its own often very individual style, there is one common thread: a genuine appreciation of the importance of good food as a basic commodity, with a blessed absence of pretension or snobbery. What more could you ask for?

SOPHIE GRIGSON

Extremadura
SPAIN

Soups
Gazpacho Chilled Tomato Soup   p.14
Sopa de Tomate Extremeña Hot Tomato Soup with Egg   p.15

Starters and Small Dishes
Revuelto de Triguero Scrambled Eggs with Asparagus   p.16
Escabeche de Truchas Marinated Fried Trout   p.18

Main Courses
Frito de Cordero Lamb Stew   p.19
Chuletas de Cordero con Hierbas Herbed Lamb Cutlets   p.20
Cocido Extremeño Three-course Chickpea and Pork Stew   p.20
Arroz con Conejo Rice with Rabbit   p.22
Bacalao a la Extremeña Salt Cod Extremadura-style   p.23
Hornazo Chorizo and Egg Bread   p.24

Vegetables
Patatas a la Extremeña Potato and Pepper Stew   p.25

Desserts
Tocino de Cielo Heavenly Bacon   p.28
Repapalos Sweet Bread Dumplings   p.29
Leche Frita Fried Custard   p.30

Extremadura
SPAIN

A ham cellar in Extremadura.

The Extremadura region is not on the standard tourist itinerary. It's a long drive from Madrid, a good four hours or more. A great plain in south-west central Spain, flanked by Portugal on one side, bordered by gently rising sierras to the north and south, it's horrendously hot in summer, icy cold in winter. Even its name makes it sound remote – 'the land beyond the River Duero' . . . the back of beyond. Few visitors venture into the foothills of the Sierra Morena or discover the small town of Llerena in the south-east of the region.

There's no outstanding reason why Llerena should pull in the crowds. The narrow white-washed streets are charming, but that's nothing exceptional in Spain. The Michelin guide describes the main square as 'one of the most monumental in all Extremadura', which might draw the odd passer-by for a ten-minute tea break. We'd probably never have gone there if it hadn't been for Felisa Zamorano, vice-president of the Cofradía Extremadura De La Buena Mesa (which translates literally as the Extremaduran Brotherhood of the Good Table).

For all the grandeur of her title, Felisa is anything but intimidating. She is a primary school teacher, married to Anastasio Sanchez, a now-retired butcher and livestock trader, mother of six grown-up children, and a fabulous cook. From the moment we met her, we felt comfortable and welcome, more like old friends than total strangers.

Felisa and Anastasio love their food, and she is a gold-mine of information on local traditional cooking. She learnt to cook from her two grandmothers, loving the warmth of their kitchens and the tempting smells that wafted out. Living in the country, a few miles outside Llerena, the family was almost self-sufficient, with its own olive groves for oil, a pig or two for meat, chickens and a vegetable garden. One of the few things ever bought from the market was fish from the Guadiana river, further north.

On Saturday we ate at Felisa's and Anastasio's home in Llerena, but Sunday was to be spent at Los Molinos, her childhood home. While Felisa packed lunch, Anastasio took us on a tour of the town, ostensibly to see the main sights, but an excuse, too, to pick up a few extra supplies.

Llerena was an important centre for the Inquisition, and we were shown, in the main square, the balconies above the entrance to the imposing church, from which the Inquisitors pronounced sentence; and, on the outskirts of town, the cross marking the grim spot where executions were carried out. For a while the great painter Zurbaran, local boy made good, lived in a house by the church, and to this day the bakers in the area bake loaves identical to those that appear in his paintings.

Victoria la Sorda, 'the Deaf One' – Anastasio doesn't remember her proper surname – lives in a cool shaded backstreet. The front of the house is deceptively small; inside, the tiled main corridor stretches back, bedrooms as neat as a pin on either side (Victoria showed me every last one of them, so I know), and at the back a brand-new bathroom opposite the spacious kitchen.

Throughout our tour of the town, I'd been clutching a 2-litre plastic jar, firmly thrust into my hands by Felisa. At last its purpose was revealed. Victoria and her husband, a vigorous old man of eighty-two, own a sizeable olive grove just outside the town walls. He picks the olives and she cures them here in her back yard. From a big, blue, plastic bin in the kitchen she ladles the cracked greenish-mauve olives into our jar.

The back yard comes as quite a surprise. Clustered around a courtyard are several small outhouses: one for a goat, one for a calf, one for curing the olives and drying herbs and peppers. There's a well – Victoria won't use tap water for the curing, what with all the chemicals in it. Well water and rain water are far better. Through an arch there's a tiny walled garden, almost a field, for growing vegetables and fodder.

Next door but one lives Manuel Cavo. Manuel used to be a *recovero* (that's the local word; it's *recadero* in general Spanish), until a few years ago when the motorcar finally ruined his trade. He would travel around the villages and isolated farmhouses, taking orders for this or that, finding out what they had surpluses of as well as what they needed. Returning to town he would make the purchases, or arrange exchanges of goods with other villagers, then deliver them back to those in want. Though money was involved in some of the transactions, the bulk of it was barter and Manuel was often paid in kind.

There was one more stop to make, at the convent a few doors up from Felisa's and Anastasio's house. Earlier that morning I'd heard the nuns singing in the church, hidden away behind an intricate screen. This is a closed order. As is common in Spain, Italy and Portugal, the nuns here are master (or should that be 'mistress'?) confectioners, turning out a wide range of cakes and sweets.

On one side of the scruffy courtyard is a door leading to a small room with a turntable in one corner and a lengthy price list tacked up beside it. Though they make all kinds of goodies, from choux pastry eclairs to rusk-like biscuits, the nuns' speciality is *yemas*, egg-yolk sweets. The production of *yemas* is a widespread practice that arose largely in wine-making areas (just up the road in Almendralejo, a desperately ugly town, they make some superb wines). Egg whites were once used to clarify wine, and the yolks were charitably passed on to the nuns. Llerena's nuns are most renowned for their *corazones*, pretty, heart-shaped, egg-yolk and almond biscuits, though I have to admit a sneaking preference for the little squares of *tocino de cielo*, heavenly bacon. How could you resist a name like that?

Purchases and sight-seeing completed, we trailed back to the house to find Felisa sitting waiting surrounded by an endless assortment of plastic foodboxes. These contained a few odd provisions for lunch – enough to keep an army marching for weeks. We just about managed to squeeze the whole lot and ourselves into their car and we were off, to spend the rest of the day under the olive trees, eating and drinking in the soft spring air.

Jamón Jamón

In Spanish Extremadura there exists a race of pig, the *Cerdo iberico*, that has been whiffling about the plains for many thousands of years and has, thankfully, largely escaped remodelling to a breed of super-pig. This pig really lives. It is happiest rootling around the holm oak and cork trees of the *dehesa* (the word used to describe the typical countryside of the region), munching *bellotas* (acorns). What's more, it is actually free to wander about and exercise those legs that will, in time, become the famous *jamón serrano* (air-dried ham) of Extremadura.

Well adapted to the dry awesome plains, these pigs flourish where others simply expire. But the breed is more than just a living relic; it has a vital role to play in local life. If the pigs do well, the farmers are, in turn, assured of a decent income, and – in principle, at least – everyone is happy. The local farmers have become well aware that it is in their interest to protect the breed, especially after a porcine disease from Africa temporarily devastated the population in the late 1960s.

Although it has a slower rate of growth than other pigs, there is one important biological reason why the hams of the *Cerdo iberico* taste so superb. It all comes down to that deeply unfashionable item: fat. The key is its distribution within the muscle for, however unappetizing it may sound, this is what gives flavour to the meat – lean meat tastes bland. Here their well-exercised haunches and the diet rich in acorns are two vital ingredients. But there's a third, and that's the quality of the air. The very best hams are cured and dried in Jabugo, a delightful town that sits just past the border between Extremadura and Andalucia, where the air is deemed to be perfect for the process of drying and maturation, which can take many years.

If these Jabugo hams are labelled with a red tag, they are guaranteed to originate from pigs raised entirely on the *dehesa*, and are extremely expensive and quite exquisite. But don't rush out looking for one: they are eaten almost exclusively in Spain where, it has to be said, a proper understanding of what makes a good ham has created a sincere and passionate demand. In fact, in one of Europe's more fortunate anomalies, the best hams are not even allowed to be imported into other countries within the EU. It is said that as they cannot be raised in the aseptic surrounds of 'approved premises' we should, by implication, be protected from the deadly threat of exquisite ham. The law's a pig.

Ⓥ

Gazpacho
Chilled Tomato Soup

At Los Molinos, Felisa showed me an old wooden bowl for making Gazpacho, smoothed and sculpted through years of pounding. She still uses it to serve iced Gazpacho in, during the hottest summer days when no one can contemplate eating anything heavier.

Gazpacho, the 'liquid salad', is a soup I never tire of. Pounding it by hand is a long tedious job, but with a processor preparing it is a matter of minutes. Remember that the proportions of vegetables and other ingredients that I give below are there merely to serve as a starting point. Tomatoes, peppers, garlic and all will vary in flavour from one batch to another, so it's important to keep tasting and to adjust the seasonings to compensate for any inadequacies. To intensify both the tomato flavour and colour of the soup you can replace some of the water with tomato juice, or add a tablespoon or two of tomato purée.

SERVES 6

1½ lb (750 g) ripe, richly flavoured tomatoes, skinned, deseeded and roughly chopped
¾ cucumber, peeled and roughly chopped
1 large green pepper, deseeded and roughly chopped
½ red onion, chopped

2–2½ tablespoons red wine vinegar
5 tablespoons olive oil
4 oz (100 g) fresh white breadcrumbs
2 cloves garlic, roughly chopped (optional)
½–1 teaspoon sugar
salt and pepper

Any or all of the following to serve

diced, deseeded tomato
diced cucumber
diced red onion
diced green pepper
diced *jamón serrano*

Put all ingredients in a processor with a small slurp of iced water. Process to a fairly smooth sludge (you may have to do this in 2 batches if your processor bowl is small). Gradually stir in enough water to give a soupy consistency, 10–15 fl oz (300–450 ml) should do it. Taste and adjust the seasoning, adding a little more salt, vinegar or sugar as necessary to highlight the flavours.

Chill, and adjust the seasoning again just before serving. Place all the garnishes in small bowls and pass around for people to help themselves.

Ⓥ
Sopa de Tomate Extremeña
Hot Tomato Soup with Egg

This tomato soup is, without doubt, for cooler months. It's a comforting soup, streaked with egg and thickened with bread – economical and nourishing, and it tastes good.

SERVES 6

1 onion, chopped
2 cloves garlic, chopped
4 tablespoons olive oil
2 green peppers, deseeded and cut into thin strips
2 lb (900 g) tomatoes, skinned, deseeded and chopped

2 tablespoons tomato purée
1 level teaspoon caster sugar
1½ pints (900 ml) stock or water
½ teaspoon cumin seeds, crushed
salt and pepper

To finish

2 cloves garlic, crushed
3 eggs
2 slices of stale bread, torn into rough pieces

Fry the onion and garlic gently in the oil until golden. Add the peppers and tomatoes and continue to cook gently, stirring occasionally, until very thick – a good 20 minutes or more. Now add the tomato purée, sugar, stock, cumin, salt and pepper. Bring to the boil and simmer for 15 minutes. Stir in the crushed garlic and draw off the heat. Immediately break in the eggs and add the stale bread. Stir, cover and allow to sit for 5 minutes. Taste and adjust the seasoning, then serve.

Ⓥ

Revuelto de Triguero
Scrambled Eggs with Asparagus

Revuelto de Triguero *or, to give it its full name,* Huevos Revueltos con Espárragos Trigueros *somehow seems to sum up the cooking of the Extremadura. It is a very simple dish, improved scrambled eggs, the sort that is only worth making with classy quality ingredients. Most households, however impoverished, would have had eggs from their chickens, a cured ham (made in the spring when their annual pig was slaughtered) hanging from the rafters, olive oil from their olive tree, garlic from the garden.* Espárragos trigueros *is the wild asparagus that grows between the rows of wheat in the fields, free for the taking.*

Wild asparagus, with its slightly bitter flavour, is something worth hunting down, as long as you take care to identify it properly. Assuming, however, that none is immediately available to you, I'd suggest that you replace it with the thinnest asparagus that you can buy, which should be labelled 'sprue'.

Not that you have to have asparagus to make an Extremaduran Revuelto. Below I give just a few of the many variations that we came across. The best one is, I'm afraid, based on another elusive ingredient, criadillos, *the poor man's truffle, a kind of tuber that grows wild in the region.*

SERVES 4

8 oz (225 g) wild or thin sprue asparagus
8 eggs, beaten
1 tablespoon white wine vinegar
salt and pepper
3 tablespoons olive oil

3 cloves garlic, sliced
1 bay leaf
2 oz (50 g) *jamón serrano*, cut into strips
   (optional)

Cut the asparagus into 1-inch (2.5-cm) lengths, discarding the tough bits at the end of the stems. Beat the eggs with the vinegar, salt and pepper.

Warm the oil in a wide frying-pan. Add the garlic and fry until golden, then take out and discard. Turn the heat down very low and add the asparagus and bay leaf, stir, then cover and sweat gently for 5–10 minutes, until tender, stirring occasionally. If using *jamón serrano*, add it to the pan when the asparagus is half-cooked.

Uncover and add the beaten eggs. Stir and scramble until the eggs have thickened, but are still moist. Serve immediately.

Variations

Add a pinch of crushed cumin seeds to the beaten eggs before pouring into the pan. Sometimes the dish is stretched by including cubes of crisply fried bread.

Instead of asparagus, mushrooms can be used. Fry them in the oil, uncovered, over a brisk heat to evaporate off their liquid, then reduce the heat and continue as above.

Another alternative is to replace the asparagus with shredded leek, adding, if you wish, a few whole cloves of garlic that have been pre-cooked in boiling water.

Swiss chard, spinach and cabbage all need to be blanched in boiling water before being stewed for a few minutes in the oil.

Escabeche de Truchas
Marinated Fried Trout

Fresh fish may have been a rarity in this part of the Extremadura, but every now and then it might be bought from the market or fished a few miles away in one of the burbling streams of the foothills of the Sierra Morena. As a result it was treated with great respect, cooked carefully with only the best of spices and aromatics. Preservation was of utmost importance if it wasn't to be eaten immediately.

This Escabeche *fulfils all requirements. The fried fish is marinated with enough vinegar to preserve it for a few days, without overwhelming the delicate flavour. Golden saffron, cloves, bay leaves and oranges scent the flesh.*

SERVES 4–8

4 small trout, scaled and cleaned	seasoned flour
salt and pepper	olive oil for frying
4 cloves garlic	2 oranges
1 bay leaf	6 cloves
generous pinch of saffron threads	4 tablespoons white wine vinegar

Cut the heads and fins off the fish. Season inside and out with salt and pepper, then leave in a cool place for 2 hours.

Heat a heavy iron griddle or frying-pan over a high flame until searingly hot. Lay the garlic in it and reduce the heat slightly. Roast the garlic, turning occasionally, until black on the outside but soft inside. Set aside.

Quickly toast the bay leaf, turning once and whipping it out before it can burn. Toast the saffron threads for a few seconds, then scrape out into a mortar. Crush the bay leaf and saffron threads to as fine a powder as possible. Peel the cloves of garlic and add the pulp to the mortar. Pound to a smooth paste. Sieve to remove the fibres, and reserve.

Coat the trout in seasoned flour, then fry in hot olive oil, turning once, until just cooked. Lay in a non-metallic dish (Felisa always uses earthenware for this) that takes the fish snugly with little room to spare. Slice the oranges, skin and all, then stick the cloves into some of the slices and lay over the fish. Sprinkle with half the vinegar. Dilute the garlic paste with a little water and spoon over, then add enough water barely to cover the fish. Taste and see if you think it needs a little more vinegar to sharpen up, though the vinegar shouldn't be too intrusive. Cover and leave to marinate in the refrigerator for at least 24 hours before serving.

Frito de Cordero
Lamb Stew

The lamb in the Extremadura is so good that it needs little seasoning to bring out the flavour. Felisa never adds any herbs to this lamb stew. Back home in England I've found that sneaking a sprig of thyme in with the lamb as it cooks is no bad thing.

The stew is thickened with a pounded paste of fried onion, garlic and bread, added towards the end of the cooking time, which gives a rich thick sauce that just coats the lamb.

SERVES 4

2 lb (900 g) boned leg of lamb, trimmed
4 tablespoons olive oil
½ onion, chopped
4–5 cloves garlic, sliced
1 bay leaf
1 slice of stale bread, crusts removed

1 teaspoon Spanish paprika (*pimentón*)
pinch of chilli powder
4 fl oz (120 ml) red wine
salt and pepper
1 sprig of fresh thyme (optional)

Cut the lamb into pieces about 2 × 3 inches (5 × 7.5 cm). They can be bigger (as Anastasio likes them), in which case they'll be pinker in the middle, or smaller (as Felisa's mother likes them), in which case the meat will end up well-done all the way through. Trim off the excess fat and any gristle.

Heat the oil in a wide saucepan or deep frying-pan. Add the onion, garlic and bay leaf and fry gently until the onion is tender and golden. Discard the bay leaf. Scoop the onion and garlic out into a mortar (or small grinder) and pound to a paste. In the same oil (add a little more if you need to) fry the bread over a medium heat until nicely browned and crisp. Break the bread into the onion/garlic mixture, then pound it in, to form *el machado*, the pounded mixture that will thicken the sauce at the end of the cooking time. If you have a processor that can handle small quantities, onion, garlic and bread can all be whizzed up together.

Take the pan off the heat while you are busy pounding and stir the paprika and chilli powder into the oil, followed by the meat. Return to a gentle heat and pour in the wine. Season with salt and pepper, and add the thyme (if using). Cover tightly and cook over a very low heat, stirring occasionally, until the meat is tender – about 10–15 minutes. Stir in the *machado* and simmer for another 5 minutes or so, by which the sauce should be thick and moist, but not runny. Adjust the seasoning and serve.

Chuletas de Cordero con Hierbas
Herbed Lamb Cutlets

Both garden herbs and the exquisitely perfumed wild herbs, from the dehesa, *are used to scent the already beautifully flavoured lamb that is reared in the Extremadura.*

Rosemary, thyme and oregano give grilled lamb cutlets a hint of their scent. Marinate them for as long as you can, pressing the herbs into the meat every now and then.

SERVES 4

8–12 lamb cutlets, depending on size
4 tablespoons olive oil
4 tablespoons dry white wine
1 tablespoon fresh rosemary leaves

2 teaspoons fresh thyme leaves
1 heaped teaspoon dried oregano
2 cloves garlic, crushed
salt and pepper

Marinate the cutlets with all the remaining ingredients for at least 24 hours, turning every now and then. Brush the extraneous debris off the cutlets, then grill them fairly close to the heat source for about 3–5 minutes on each side, depending on how well you like them done and how hot the grill is. Serve immediately.

Cocido Extremeño
Three-course Chickpea and Pork Stew

Cocido *is perhaps the most ubiquitous of Spanish stews, made all over the country, though it varies considerably from one area to another. In the Extremadura it is made with chickpeas, as well as lots of meats including the marvellous chorizos and morcillas (black puddings) of the region. Some people include chicken. At the time of the* matanza, *when the pigs are slaughtered, their ears, tails and ribs – parts that can't be used for sausages or cured – may also go into the cauldron.*

As with the French poule-au-pot *and the Portuguese* caldeirada, *one huge cooking pot is used to produce several courses. The broth is served first, followed by the chickpeas and finally the meat: a perfect party dish.*

Felisa likes to serve a clean simple lettuce salad after the meats, while others accompany the meats with a finely diced salsa *of seeded tomatoes, green peppers and red onions, dressed with vinegar and olive oil.*

SERVES 6–8

12 oz (350 g) chickpeas, soaked in water overnight

2 lb (900 g) veal bones

1½ lb (750 g) shin of beef

8 oz (225 g) belly of pork with rind

8 oz (225 g) piece of smoked streaky bacon with rind, or 1 smoked pork knuckle

8 oz (225 g) piece of cooking *chorizo* (don't slice or skin)

8 oz (225 g) piece of *morcilla* or black pudding (don't slice or skin)

8 oz (225 g) tomatoes, halved

3 carrots, quartered

½ Savoy cabbage, shredded

1 lb (450 g) potatoes, peeled and cut into 2-inch (5-cm) chunks (optional)

salt and pepper

To finish the broth

4 cloves garlic, sliced

3 tablespoons chopped fresh parsley

2 tablespoons white wine vinegar

3 sprigs of fresh mint

2 slices of stale bread, torn into small pieces

Drain and rinse the chickpeas and put into a huge pan with the veal bones, shin of beef, belly of pork and bacon. Add 8 pints (4.5 litres) water and bring to the boil. Boil hard for 5 minutes, skim off the scum, then reduce the heat and simmer very gently for 2 hours.

Now add the *chorizo*, *morcilla*, all the vegetables except the potatoes, salt and pepper. Continue simmering for a further 1 hour. Add the potatoes (if using) about 15 minutes before the stew is cooked.

Carefully lift out the meats, vegetables and potatoes (if used). Place in a serving dish and spoon over a little of the broth to prevent them drying out. Keep warm, covered, in the oven. Next scoop out all the chickpeas into a bowl, again adding a couple of ladlefuls of the broth to keep them moist. Cover and keep warm in the oven.

Strain the broth into a clean pan, add the garlic, parsley, vinegar and mint. Simmer for 5 minutes, then taste and adjust the seasoning. Add the bread, cover and let it soak for another 2–3 minutes, then serve.

Once the soup has been eaten, bring on the chickpeas, which are usually eaten from the same bowls, semi-mashed into any remaining broth. Finally the bowls are cleared away, to be replaced with clean plates for the meats.

Arroz con Conejo
Rice with Rabbit

This is not a risotto, nor a paella either for that matter. It is a full-flavoured rice and rabbit stew, homely to look at (I can't deny that it has a somewhat murky aspect), but nevertheless very good to eat.

Felisa makes the stew in two stages. When she has a moment during the early part of the day, she simmers the rabbit until very tender, making sure that there is plenty of liquid in the pan. Twenty minutes or so before serving, she re-heats it, adding the rice, so that it is perfectly cooked by the time everyone has gathered around the table.

SERVES 4–6

1 rabbit, cut into small pieces
3 tablespoons olive oil
½ onion, chopped
5 cloves garlic, peeled but whole
1 green pepper, chopped
1 bay leaf
1 large tomato weighing about 8 oz
    (225 g), skinned, seeded and chopped
2 tablespoons chopped fresh parsley
1 generous glass white or red wine
salt and pepper
8 oz (225 g) medium-grain rice

Brown the rabbit in the olive oil in a wide shallow pan, then remove it from the pan and set aside. Add the onion, 3 of the whole garlic cloves, the green pepper and the bay leaf to the pan and cook gently until the onion and pepper are tender. Now return the rabbit to the pan, together with the tomato and parsley. Stir and cook for 5 minutes. Pour in the wine and enough water to cover the rabbit generously, and add salt and pepper. Bring to the boil and simmer gently, covered, for about 1 hour, until the rabbit is very tender. There should still be loads of liquid in the pan. Taste and adjust the seasonings.

Stir the rice into the liquid and simmer, stirring occasionally, for 10–20 minutes, until the rice. is tender. When it is almost done, crush the remaining 2 garlic cloves and stir into the rice.

When the rice is cooked, it will have absorbed a considerable amount of liquid, but the dish should still be fairly soupy and wet – if necessary add a little extra water or stock. Serve immediately.

Bacalao a la Extremeña
Salt Cod Extremadura-style

Though fresh fish was something of a rarity, salt cod could be kept, and was always available, though by no means cheap. This is Felisa's way of cooking it, fried first, then submerged in a tomato and pepper sauce, flavoured, as are so many of the local dishes, with bay leaves and garlic.

A word of warning: make sure that all the windows are open and that the extractor fan, if you have one, is set on high when you fry the cod. It is a mite on the smelly side.

SERVES 4–6

1½ lb (750 g) best-quality salt cod, soaked in water for 24 hours (see p.214)
flour
1 egg, beaten
4–5 tablespoons olive oil
1 onion, chopped
2 cloves garlic, chopped
2 green peppers, diced

1 lb (450 g) tomatoes, skinned, seeded and roughly chopped
10 fl oz (300 ml) *passata*
2 bay leaves
1 tablespoon tomato purée
1 teaspoon sugar
salt and pepper

Drain the salt cod and place in a shallow pan with just enough water to cover. Bring slowly to the boil, draw off the heat, cover and leave to cool. Drain thoroughly. Cut the cod into large chunks, 1½–2 inches (4–5 cm) square, give or take, discarding the bones and skin. Coat in flour (don't add any extra salt), then dip into egg, and coat again, thoroughly, in flour. Fry in hot oil until golden-brown all over. Drain on kitchen paper.

Warm 3 tablespoons oil in a fairly capacious pan. Add the onion, garlic and peppers and cook gently until tender without browning. Now add all the remaining ingredients (but no salt yet), bring to a simmer and simmer for about 30 minutes to make a thick sauce. Add the fried cod, and simmer for a further 5 minutes. Taste and add salt if needed. Serve piping hot.

Hornazo
Chorizo and Egg Bread

This is the impressively grand Extremadura answer to the sausage roll – on a big scale, and with whole baked eggs thrown in into the bargain. Felisa orders Hornazos *from the baker in a nearby village, Valverde de Llerena, when she is organizing a picnic.*

The bread is filled with a whole hoop of chorizo. *As it bakes, some of the fat seeps out into the dough, staining it flaming orange-red and flavouring it right through. It's best eaten on the day it is made, still warm from the oven, but it will keep for a day or so after.*

SERVES 6–8

1 oz (25 g) fresh yeast or ½ oz (15 g) dried
   yeast
1 teaspoon caster sugar
1½ lb (750 g) strong white bread flour
½ tablespoon salt

2 tablespoons olive oil
1 horseshoe-shaped cooking *chorizo* or
   about 10–12 oz (275–350 g) linked
   small cooking *chorizos*
4 eggs

Cream the yeast and sugar with about 5 fl oz (150 ml) warm water. Leave in a warm place for 10 minutes or so until frothing. Sift the flour with the salt, make a well in the centre and add the yeast mixture and olive oil. Gradually mix in another 5 fl oz (150 ml) warm water (you may need a little extra) to form a soft, slightly sticky dough. Knead vigorously for 10 minutes, then return to the bowl, dust lightly with flour and cover with a damp tea-towel. Leave in a warm place for 1–1½ hours, until doubled in bulk. Punch down and knead again for 5 minutes, then divide in half.

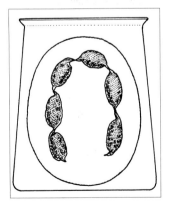

1 Roll out the dough into an oval roughly 10 × 12 inches (25 × 30 cm). Lay the *chorizo* on the dough leaving a 2 inch (5 cm) border.

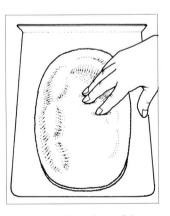

2 Moisten the edges of the dough around the *chorizo* and lay the second piece of dough on top.

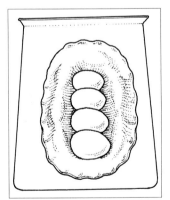

3 Press down the edges of the dough and the inner gap of the horseshoe. Brush the central dip with water and press in the whole eggs, still in their shells.

On a floured board, roll out half the dough to form a large oval about 2 inches (5 cm) bigger all the way round than the horseshoe of *chorizo* (or the links when laid in an oval shape). My dough measured roughly 12 × 10 inches (30 × 25 cm). Place the dough on a floured baking tray. Snip any string or metal tags off the *chorizo* (but don't separate the links, or skin it) and lay it on the bread dough.

Roll out the remaining dough to form an oval of the same size as the first. Moisten the dough around the *chorizo* with water, including the inner gap. Lay the second oval of dough on top and press down firmly to seal all around the *chorizo*. Brush the central dip in the middle of the *chorizo* with a little more water and press the whole eggs, still in their shells, gently down into the dip so that they sit in a nice neat row. Leave in a warm place for a further 30 minutes or so.

Pre-heat the oven to 350°F (180°C), gas mark 4. Bake the *hornazo* in the oven for 35 – 40 minutes. Tap the underneath – if it sounds hollow, it is cooked. Cool on a wire rack.

Patatas a la Extremeña
Potato and Pepper Stew

This makes a perfect supper dish, as long as you can get good chorizo *to enliven the mixture of potatoes and peppers.*

SERVES 4

2½ lb (1.25 kg) potatoes	1 green pepper, seeded and diced
3 tablespoons olive oil	2 cloves garlic, crushed
4 oz (100 g) cooking *chorizo*, skinned and roughly sliced	½ tablespoon Spanish paprika (*pimentón*)
	1 bay leaf
1 red pepper, seeded and diced	salt and pepper

Peel the potatoes and cut into roughly 1-inch (2.5 cm) chunks.

Warm the oil over a moderate heat in an earthenware *cazuela* or a wide heavy frying-pan. Add the *chorizo* and fry briskly until lightly browned. It will fall to pieces, but this doesn't matter. Reduce the heat and add all the remaining ingredients. Pour over just enough water to cover. Bring to the boil and simmer, stirring occasionally, for 20 – 30 minutes, until the potatoes are cooked and the liquid has reduced by about half. Taste and adjust the seasoning. Serve with plenty of good bread to mop up the juices.

OVERLEAF
Background: *Hornazo* (Chorizo and Egg Bread) see p.24.
Foreground: *Repapalos* (Sweet Bread Dumplings) see p.29.

Ⓥ
Tocino de Cielo
Heavenly Bacon

This is one of the best of all the yemas *(egg-yolk sweets) that abound in Spain and Portugal (where this is known as* Toucinho do Céu. *It varies in thickness from one establishment to another, may be served up in neat squares (this is how they sell it at the convent in Llerena) or turned out of little round moulds, with or without caramel. Essentially, however, this 'heavenly bacon' is a sweet, sticky, baked custard made with sugar syrup rather than cream or milk. In texture it is as smooth and silky as a baby's bottom. Very rich, undoubtedly very wicked and very delicious.*

SERVES 6–8

10 oz (275 g) caster sugar
4 strips of lemon zest
10 egg yolks, lightly beaten

Caramel

4 oz (100 g) caster sugar

Begin with the caramel. Put the sugar into a heavy-bottomed pan with 3 tablespoons water. Stir constantly over a low–medium heat until the sugar has completely dissolved, without ever letting it boil. Brush down any crystals stuck to the side of the pan with a brush dipped in cold water. Once the syrup is clear, stop stirring. Bring to the boil and boil until the syrup caramelizes to a rich brown. Watch over it carefully, and occasionally tilt the pan, gently swirling the sugar syrup, but don't be tempted to stir. Once it has caramelized, pour the syrup either into a 7-inch (18-cm) square tin, tilting to coat the base thoroughly, or into 6 small dariole moulds.

To make the syrup for the *Tocino*, put the sugar into a pan with 5 fl oz (150 ml) water and the lemon zest and stir over a medium heat until the sugar has completely dissolved without letting it boil. Brush down any crystals clinging to the side of the pan with a brush dipped in cold water. Once the syrup is clear, bring to the boil, then remove the lemon zest. Boil the syrup until it reaches 234°F (112°C), the thread stage. Use a sugar thermometer as a guide if you have one, then test by dipping 2 spoons, held back to back, into the syrup. Quickly lift out and gently pull apart. If long threads of sugar form, you've hit the right point. Quickly take the syrup off the heat and allow it to cool for about 3–4 minutes.

Pre-heat the oven to 325°F (160°C), gas mark 3.

Pour the syrup slowly into the beaten egg yolks, beating constantly with a whisk or fork. Strain the mixture into the tin or moulds coated in caramel and cover with foil. Stand in a roasting tin and pour in enough boiling water to come about half-way up the tin or mould. Bake in the oven until just set, about 30−40 minutes. Cool in the roasting tin.

When cool, turn out of the moulds (if using). If cooked in one tin, cut into squares.

Ⓥ

Repapalos
Sweet Bread Dumplings

An unexpectedly delicious pudding made for us by Felisa. William liked it so much that he took a helping for lunch, supper and lunch again the next day! The small bread dumplings are first fried, then simmered in plentiful milk: strange but, I promise you, well worth trying. Make them a day in advance − they improve with a good soak − and serve chilled, in bowls, with plenty of the cinnamon and orange-scented milk.

SERVES 8

4 oz (100 g) stale breadcrumbs (made from bread that is 2−4 days old, crust included)
4−5 large eggs, lightly beaten
olive oil, or a mixture of olive and sunflower oil, for deep-frying

3 pints (1.75 litres) full-cream milk
zest of 1 orange, cut in wide strips
2 cinnamon sticks
4 oz (100 g) caster sugar
ground cinnamon

Beat the breadcrumbs with enough of the beaten eggs to form a thick batter of dropping consistency. Let it rest for 30 minutes.

Heat the oil to 330°F (165°C) − at this temperature a piece of bread dropped into the oil should fizz gently. Test the batter by cooking one experimental dumpling. Drop a generous teaspoon of the mixture into the oil and fry for 2−4 minutes until golden. It should puff up slightly to form a nice, fairly neatly shaped ball or sphere. If it stays irredeemably lumpy and over-solid, add a little more egg to the batter to loosen it. If it disintegrates, thicken the batter with a few more breadcrumbs.

Once the batter is right, start frying seriously, as above, dropping teaspoons of it into the hot oil and turning the dumplings so that they cook evenly. Never over-crowd the pan. Drain thoroughly on kitchen paper.

Put the cooled *Repapalos* into a clean pan and add all the remaining ingredients except the ground cinnamon. Bring to the boil and simmer for 15 minutes. Spoon the dumplings into a bowl, pour the hot milk over them, dust with ground cinnamon and leave to cool. Serve chilled (I think they improve with a day or so's keeping).

ⓥ
Leche Frita
Fried Custard

Leche Frita *means, literally, fried milk, but this is in fact fried custard, a favourite Spanish pudding. The custard is made so thick that it sets solid when cooled. Cut into diamond shapes, it is coated in breadcrumbs and fried golden-brown.*

Make the custard well in advance (even the day before) so that it has plenty of time to cool down. Leave the frying to the very last minute so that everyone gets their Leche Frita *piping hot from the pan. In Spain the diamonds are usually served with a dusting of icing sugar and cinnamon. I usually do without the icing sugar since they are already pretty sweet, but the cinnamon is indispensable.*

SERVES 6

1 pint (600 ml) full-cream milk
4 strips of lemon zest
1 cinnamon stick
2 eggs plus 3 egg yolks

4 oz (100 g) caster sugar
2½ oz (65 g) cornflour
½ oz (15 g) butter

To finish

1 egg, beaten
breadcrumbs
oil for frying
icing sugar (optional)
ground cinnamon

To make the custard, bring the milk to the boil with the lemon zest and cinnamon stick. Reduce the heat as low as possible and simmer for 5 minutes. Meanwhile, in a separate pan, whisk the eggs and yolks with the sugar until pale, then whisk in the cornflour a tablespoon at a time. Pour in a splash of the hot milk, stir well, then gradually stir in the remaining milk with the cinnamon stick and lemon zest. Add the butter and return to the heat.

Bring to the boil, stirring constantly, and then simmer gently for about 1 minute. Remove the cinnamon stick and lemon zest and beat to smooth out the worst of the lumps – the custard doesn't have to be absolutely satin-smooth. Pour into an oiled dish about 8 inches (20 cm) square, to give a depth of about ½ inch (1 cm), and smooth down. Leave to cool, then chill in the refrigerator.

Just before serving, cut into 2-inch (5-cm) diamond shapes or squares. Dip into the beaten egg and coat evenly in breadcrumbs. Pour a layer of oil about ½ inch (1 cm) deep into a frying-pan, heat, and then fry the squares of custard until golden-brown. Drain briefly on kitchen paper, dust lightly with icing sugar (if you have a sweet tooth) and cinnamon and serve.

Sesimbra and the Costa Azul
PORTUGAL

Sesimbra and the Costa Azul
PORTUGAL

Sesimbra's great charm is that it is mercifully short of tourist attractions. A small hard-working town, jam-packed into the cleft of a steep valley, hard against the sea shore, it is pleasantly pretty but no great shakes on the scenic score. Of its ten thousand or so inhabitants, some three thousand – almost a third of the population – make their living from the sea, as fishermen or in jobs closely connected with the boats, port and fish trade.

Go for a stroll along the sandy beach in the early morning, and the *raison d'être* of the town is evident. Sesimbra owes its existence to the sea and dotted here and there, from the port at one end to the rocks at the other, are clusters of fishermen unravelling their twisted lines after a night of fishing. Their haul is already unloaded at the port and now being sorted, packed on ice and sent off to market.

Not surprisingly the mainstay of the Sesimbran diet is fish. In the evenings the string of restaurants along the front offers some of the wealth of the day's catch, most of it barbecued. In their homes most of the townspeople will also be dining on fish. Saturday lunchtime brings the cooking out on to the streets, with tiny portable barbecues dotting the pavements in front of many a house and the tantalizing smell of grilling sardines wafting through the alleys.

Laura Reis, our guide, and other Sesimbrans too, showed us the 'proper' way to eat a grilled sardine. Knives and forks are out and so too is lemon juice. The fish are crusted with coarse salt before grilling and eaten the moment they are done. You take a large slice of bread, slap the sardine on it and pick away the burning-hot flesh with your fingers until nothing is left but the bone and the head, which are discarded. A freshly-grilled sardine takes the place of the old one and is eaten in the same way. After two or three the bread is deliciously soaked in sardine juices, perhaps too soggy to take another load, so it's time to eat that as well and to lick your fingers clean in anticipation of another round.

Sardines and a little silvery horse-mackerel are common fare, ten a penny. A visit to the busy port or the covered market in the centre of the town reveals a much wider, fascinating range of local fish. Laura pointed out the most highly esteemed, not only here but throughout Portugal, which is the burnished silver

Bacalhau: 'O Fiel Amigo'

Cast your eye about a Portuguese fish market and the one thing you will almost certainly not see is fresh cod. Here, in the warmer waters of southern Europe, it is a rare visitor, preferring instead to live and breed in the icy coldness of the Arctic oceans. So how then, in its salted form at least, did it become such an important part of Portuguese national culture?

During the sixteenth century the Portuguese, amongst others, travelled northwards and discovered the phenomenally rich waters off the coast of what has become known as Newfoundland, *La Terre Neuve*. Here cod were so plentiful that they could be hauled out of the water in buckets. The discovery of these fishing grounds, the Grand Banks, fuelled an international industry that fed the growing European empires on a cheap and plentiful fish.

Portugal, as did France, had one great advantage in this trade, namely a ready supply of sea salt from the well-established coastal saltings, and today Sesimbran and Ibizan (Spanish) salt are still preferred by the fish processors who supply the Portuguese markets with *bacalhau* (salt cod).

In the past the wooden fishing boats would set off, laden with salt, for the foggy cold fishing grounds off Newfoundland. As soon as the cod were landed, they would be prepared for salting, gutted and cleaned, their heads making a ready meal in themselves. Most of the fish would be salted in the hold and finished off back home, where racks and sheds would be full of cod drying off in the sun, punctuating the air with that very particular *bacalhau* smell.

Both Portugal and Spain were deeply influenced by a rigorous form of Catholicism; it had, after all, largely inspired the Portuguese to try to conquer the world in the name of Christianity. *Bacalhau* became the essential – although often unaffordable – food for fast days (which included Friday, the day of the crucifixion) and Lent, as eating fish was thought to encourage spiritual reflection and was far less dangerous than the consumption of meat which might inspire lusty and often distinctly unchristian 'carnal' thoughts. This association of fish with Friday has had a long-lasting effect on many of us, but at the time the Church must have been quietly relieved that such an easily transportable food as salt cod was available, one that could be sent to the furthest corners of the empire with little danger of spoiling. The Portuguese have developed a deep attachment to *bacalhau*, referring to it at times quite simply, and most endearingly, as '*o fiel amigo*' (the faithful friend).

Two Portuguese fishermen with scabbard fish.

scabbard fish, flat and elongated (they can reach more than 3 feet (1 metre) in length) as the scabbard of their name suggests. Squid and cuttlefish abound, among the monkfish and red mullet and other stranger fish that I (and occasionally even William) failed to recognize.

In the fruit and vegetable section of the market, bunches of leafy coriander vied for space with other herbs – mint, parsley and bay leaves (branches of fresh bay are bought for drying only as the dried leaves are considered immensely superior in flavour). The use of coriander leaf, as opposed to the seed, is a European anomaly. Though the plant is native to the Mediterranean, other countries prefer the dried seeds with their aromatic orange flavour. In Portugal the leaf is among the most widely used of herbs, adding its strange taste to soups and stews.

The big news on the culinary front round here is the fishermen's stew, *caldeirada*, which really is made by the fishermen themselves. Laura introduced us to the Formiga Brothers' at their *logia*, the building where the nets and other paraphernalia of their fishing business are lodged and repaired. William was given a lesson in how to prepare *caldeirada* step-by-step, for twenty people. Eventually we sat down with the entire crew and family round a rough wooden table set among heaps of dusty equipment, a lean cat eyeing the heap of fishy bones that was building up as we all set about demolishing the tender fish and the even more delicious soup that followed.

Not that the cooking of fish here is limited to *caldeirada* and grilled sardines. Far from it. To prove the point Laura led us through winding back streets to a small nondescript cafe-cum-take-away. Maria-Jose Borges presides over the kitchen, while her husband Arthur and their daughter charm the customers – well, us at any rate – into eating or buying far more than they really need.

As is usual in many restaurants, the first things to arrive on the table, whether you order them or not, are a local cheese and tiny plastic pots of fish spread! In some places this may be home-made, but it's far more common to get the factory versions, which can be surprisingly palatable. The cheese, though, is the treat that starts the meal. Most of the time we ate the small hard cheeses of the nearby hills, and once we were lucky enough to get the exquisitely rich and runny *queso de Azeitão*, one of Portugal's great cheeses, made a few miles away on the edge of the wild and beautiful Arrabida national park.

At Maria-Jose's a little prompting will bring forth dishes of fried *chorizo*, fattier and with a very different flavour from that of Spain, and garlicky olives. The rest of the menu is short and simple, half a dozen or so main courses, including one special of the day, which is where her skill as a cook shines through.

On our last night in Sesimbra we dined with Laura at the smartest restaurant on the sea front, fanned by a cool sea breeze at the end of a long hot day. We ate fish baked in a salt dome, and listened to Laura's tales of her life in Sesimbra.

Though Sesimbra has been transformed in many ways during her lifetime, its heartbeat remains the same as always. It exists because of the sea. The inhabitants, as they have done for centuries, rely on the sea for their prosperity and income, for fishing, for tourism, and above all for their daily food.

Caldo Verde
Potato and Kale Soup

When I went to the market with Laura, I was fascinated by the shredding machines that sat on half a dozen of the vegetable and fruit stalls. In front of each drum was a heap of finely shredded vegetables for making soup – carrots and runner beans mixed together, white cabbage and, most common of all, threads of couve, *a green-leaved cabbage, used to make this soup. The nearest thing to* couve *that I've found here is curly kale, sturdy and dark, but spring greens, or even Savoy cabbage make fine alternatives.*

SERVES 4

1 lb (450 g) potatoes
1 clove garlic, sliced
½ small onion, finely chopped
salt and pepper

8 oz (225 g) curly kale
4 oz (100 g) *chouriço* or Spanish *chorizo*,
    sliced
4 tablespoons extra-virgin olive oil

Peel and slice the potatoes. Place in a large saucepan with the garlic, onion, salt and pepper and enough water to cover generously. Simmer until tender. Pass through the fine blade of a mouli-legume, or mash to a smooth purée. Add a little more water if necessary to thin to a soupy consistency. Return to the pan and adjust the seasoning, adding plenty of pepper.

While the potatoes are cooking, cut the stalks from the kale, then roll up the leaves and shred *very* thinly (the resulting threads of cabbage should be around ⅛ inch (3 mm) wide). Bring the soup back to the boil. Stir in the kale (that's why you needed a large pan) and sausage and simmer for 5 minutes. Ladle into 4 soup bowls, pour a tablespoon of olive oil on to each one and serve.

Ⓥ

Sopa de Coentro
Potato and Coriander Soup

This is a soup which Laura often makes in the winter months. The flavour of coriander permeates it through and through. How big is a small bunch of coriander? Well, that depends on how much you like it. My bunch would be a comfortable handful, but that may not help you a great deal. See how you feel, and how much coriander you have.

1 small bunch of coriander	2 lb (900 g) potatoes, peeled and cubed
2 onions, chopped	2 pints (1.2 litres) chicken stock or water
2 cloves garlic, chopped	salt and pepper
3 tablespoons olive oil	

Cut the stalks from the coriander and tie them in a bundle with string. Chop the leaves and reserve.

Fry the onions and garlic gently in the oil until tender without browning. Add the diced potatoes and coriander stalks, stir, then cover and sweat over a low heat for 5 minutes. Now add the stock, salt and pepper and bring to the boil. Simmer until the potatoes are very tender. Remove the bundle of coriander stalks. Pass the potatoes through a mouli-legume. You can process them instead, but only if you've got time to let them rest for a couple of hours afterwards, as processing produces a gluey texture.

Stir in the coriander leaves and re-heat gently without boiling. Serve hot.

Ⓥ
Sopa de Ervilhas e Coentro
Pea and Coriander Soup

This is a simple spring-time variation on the preceding soup, replacing some of the potato with green peas – for preference freshly shelled, but frozen ones do a perfectly acceptable job of it. Their natural sweetness is lovely with the coriander.

1 small bunch of coriander	10 oz (275 g) shelled peas (shelled weight),
2 onions, chopped	thawed if frozen
2 cloves garlic, chopped	2 pints (1.2 litres) chicken stock or water
3 tablespoons olive oil	salt and pepper
1 lb (450 g) potatoes, diced	

Make as the *Sopa de Coentro* on p.36, adding the peas to the pan with the potatoes.

Carapaus de Escabeche
Marinated Horse-mackerel

Horse-mackerel, it must be said, are not the most riveting fish in the world. In Sesimbra they are often grilled, like small sardines, but the nicest way of cooking them is as an escabeche – that is, fried and marinated, to serve cold as an hors d'oeuvre. Of course, sardines respond even better to this kind of treatment, and as you are more likely to come across them here than horse-mackerel, I suggest that is what you use.

SERVES 4–6

12 small horse-mackerel or sardines,
    scaled and cleaned
salt
3 fl oz (85 ml) sunflower or vegetable oil

Marinade

1 large onion, sliced	2 sprigs of fresh thyme
3 cloves garlic, chopped	6 black peppercorns, coarsely crushed
4 fl oz (120 ml) olive oil	1 teaspoon paprika
1 bay leaf	4 fl oz (120 ml) white wine vinegar
2 tablespoons chopped fresh parsley	salt

Season the fish with salt and leave to stand for 30 minutes. Pat dry. Fry, in several batches if necessary, in the sunflower oil over a brisk heat until just cooked. Drain briefly on kitchen paper, then lay in a shallow dish.

Place the onion, garlic and olive oil in a pan and cook over a medium–low heat until the onion is tender, without browning. Draw off the heat and stir in all the remaining ingredients. Pour over the fish and leave to marinate for at least 24 hours. Serve as a first course with plenty of bread to mop up the marinade.

Pastéis de Bacalhau
Salt Cod Croquettes

When they are freshly cooked, with a generous proportion of salt cod to potato, these croquettes are absolutely irresistible. If you've tried them in Portugal, and rejected them as far too heavy and stodgy and over-salty, then I suggest you try making your own. You'll soon notice the difference.

MAKES 16–18

8 oz (225 g) salt cod, soaked and drained (see p.214)	2 cloves garlic, finely chopped
12 oz (350 g) floury potatoes, boiled in their skins	2 tablespoons finely chopped fresh parsley
1 small onion, finely chopped	salt and pepper
	1–2 eggs, lightly beaten
	sunflower or olive oil for deep-frying

Place the salt cod in a wide pan and cover with water. Bring slowly to a quiet simmer, and simmer for 5–10 minutes depending on thickness, until it flakes easily. Drain, and flake with your fingers, discarding the skin and bones. Using a fork and your fingers, tear the fish into fine threads. Peel the potatoes and mash thoroughly or pass through the fine blade of a mouli-legume – the latter is probably the better method.

Mix the cod and potatoes with the onion, garlic, parsley, pepper and salt if needed. Add enough egg to form a cohesive stiff mass – at this stage use your hands to mix and work the paste. Let it cool completely.

Take egg-sized pieces of the mixture and, using 2 tablespoons, shape them into small rugby-ball croquettes. Deep-fry a few at a time in hot oil at 360°F (182°C), until richly browned. Drain briefly on kitchen paper and eat straight away.

If you want to re-heat any, pop them back in hot oil for a few minutes to crisp up.

Caldeirada
Rich Fish Stew

At a feast to mark St John's Eve, Senhor Domingo, a short, wiry, weather-beaten fisherman presided over the cauldrons of caldeirada *bubbling away on a two-ring portable gas stove. He's famous for his* Caldeirada *and is hauled in to cook it on many a semi-official occasion.*

It's clearly a party dish, best prepared in large quantity with lots of immaculately fresh fish. When made for twenty or more, the remarkable thing is that you have to add no extra water — the built-up layers of fish produce all that is needed. In smaller quantities — say, just enough for 6–8 — you have to use a slightly different method, boosting the liquid content with a slug of water. If you want to get ahead, prepare the stew in advance, stopping just short of adding the fish.

Caldeirada *is always served in two courses. The fish and vegetables come first, to be followed by the soup (the bit we liked best in the end), flavoured with mint and stretched with a handful of pasta.*

SERVES 6–8

3–4 lb (1.5–1.75 kg) mixed fish (conger eel, monkfish, skate, bream, etc.)

8 oz (225 g) fish livers (if you can get them), cleaned

4 fl oz (120 ml) olive oil

4 medium onions, sliced

3 cloves garlic, chopped

1½ lb (750 g) tomatoes, skinned, seeded and roughly chopped

1 lb (450 g) potatoes, cut into ¾-inch (2-cm) dice (no larger)

1 green pepper, seeded and chopped

2 bay leaves

2 tablespoons finely chopped fresh parsley

salt and pepper

1½ pints (900 ml) *passata*

6 fl oz (175 ml) dry white wine

4 oz (100 g) stelline or other tiny pasta shapes

2 tablespoons chopped fresh mint

Cut the fish into chunks about 1½-inches (4–5 cm) thick. Rinse the fish livers, if using, and cut into pieces about 1 inch (2.5 cm) thick.

In a heavy pan large enough to take all the ingredients except the pasta, drizzle a generous layer of olive oil. Now build up layers of onion, garlic, tomatoes, potatoes and green pepper, tucking in the bay leaves and sprinkling with parsley as you go. Season with salt and pepper and pour over the *passata*, wine and 10 fl oz (300 ml) water. Drizzle over all except about 2 tablespoons of the remaining olive oil. Bring up to the boil and simmer for 15 minutes, stirring occasionally.

Now add the fish (but not the livers), pressing it down gently into the stew. Drizzle over the last of the oil. Cover tightly and simmer for 5 minutes. Add the livers, if using, cover again and simmer for another 5 minutes or so, until the fish is cooked.

With a slotted spoon lift out the fish, livers, potatoes and bits of pepper if you can find them. Cover and keep warm for a few minutes. Strain the sauce into a clean pan, pressing as much as you can through the sieve. Add 10 fl oz (300 ml) water, bring to the boil, then add the pasta. Leave to simmer gently while you and your guests eat the fish and potatoes. Check after 10 minutes or so, and if the pasta is cooked, draw off the heat.

Re-heat the soup, stir in the chopped mint and serve.

Bacalhau à Gomes de Sá
Salt Cod with Potatoes and Olives

This is quite possibly the best ever way of cooking salt cod. William and I both tucked into it gleefully when Maria Jose showed me how to make it, eating far more than was good for us. It's one of those dishes that is somehow more than the sum of its parts, a blessed blend of tastes and textures, brought together with plenty of rich olive oil – don't be tempted to reduce the quantity for the sake of a few calories.

SERVES 4–6

1 lb (450 g) salt cod, soaked and drained (see p.214)
4 eggs
4 medium potatoes, boiled in their skins
5 fl oz (150 ml) olive oil
3 cloves garlic, chopped

2 large onions, chopped
3 tablespoons finely chopped fresh parsley
salt and pepper
20 black olives

Put the salt cod and eggs (still in their shells) into a pan and add enough water to cover. Bring to the boil and simmer for 8 minutes. Remove the eggs and check on the cod to see how it is doing. If it flakes easily, drain it. If it doesn't, simmer gently for a few more minutes until it's done, then drain. Flake the cod, discarding the skin and bones. Shell the eggs and slice. Peel the cooked potatoes and cut into 1-inch (2.5 cm) chunks.

Put the olive oil and garlic into a wide deep frying-pan and warm over a gentle heat for a minute or so, then add the onions. Cook until the onions are translucent and tender, without browning. Now add the flaked salt cod, stir for a minute and add the potatoes. Continue stirring until piping hot, then stir in the parsley and pepper. Add a little salt if it is needed, but be careful as the cod may have already provided quite enough. Tip into a warm serving dish and garnish with the sliced eggs and olives. Serve immediately.

Bacalhau à Brás
Salt Cod with Potato Straws and Egg

This is another very popular Portuguese way with salt cod, and though again it brings in potatoes, eggs and olives, it is nothing like Bacalhau à Gomes de Sá. *Here the potato is fried in matchstick-fine strips and then scrambled with the cod and eggs.*

SERVES 4–6

12 oz (350 g) salt cod, soaked and drained (see p.214)
1 lb (450 g) potatoes
sunflower oil for deep-frying
5 tablespoons olive oil
3 cloves garlic, finely chopped

2 onions, very thinly sliced
pepper
6 eggs, beaten
2 tablespoons finely chopped fresh parsley
12 black olives

Skin and bone the cod. Rinse in cold water, then pull into shreds. Pat dry with kitchen paper or a clean tea-towel.

Peel the potatoes and cut into thin matchsticks. Rinse in cold water and dry thoroughly. Deep-fry in hot sunflower oil until golden-brown – do this in several small batches rather than one big one. Drain on kitchen paper.

Put the olive oil and garlic into a wide deep frying-pan (it should be large enough to take all the ingredients eventually) and warm over a gentle heat for a minute or so, then add the onions. Cook until the onions are translucent and tender, without browning. Add the cod and continue to cook slowly for 5 minutes, stirring constantly. Quickly mix in the potatoes and pepper, then pour in the eggs and add half the parsley. Stir briefly with a fork until the eggs are creamy but not yet solid. Spoon into a serving dish, scatter with the remaining parsley and the olives. Serve immediately.

Chocos com Molho a Pé Descalço
Barefooted Cuttlefish

Maria-Jose usually cooks cuttlefish this way — it's very easy, saves fiddling about cleaning out the bodies and, of course, it tastes very good. The name comes from the dark inky colour of the sauce and the cuttlefish — the colour of the soles of bare feet after running around in the streets. If you don't fancy the comparison, the more prosaic name is Chocos com Tinta *(Cuttlefish in Ink Sauce).*

SERVES 4

4 medium cuttlefish — with bodies of
    around 3–4 inches (7.5–10 cm) long
4 tablespoons olive oil
3 cloves garlic, chopped

1 large onion, chopped
salt and pepper
1 bay leaf
5 fl oz (150 ml) white wine

Wash the cuttlefish but leave whole. Drizzle 1 tablespoon oil over the base of a heavy pan wide enough to take all the fish in a single close-packed layer.

Make a bed in the pan of 1 garlic clove and the onion, and lay the cuttlefish on top. Sprinkle over the remaining chopped garlic, season with salt and pepper and tuck the bay leaf in too. Spoon over the remaining oil and pour in the wine. Bring to a gentle simmer and half-cover.

Check after 10 minutes. By this time the white cuttles should be sticking up out of the cuttlefish and can be easily removed. Throw them out. Turn the fish over. Simmer, uncovered, for a further 5–10 minutes, until the cuttlefish is tender and bathed in a thin sauce darkened with its own ink.

Peixe Espada com Ervilhas
Scabbard Fish with Peas

Peixe espada *(scabbard fish)* is held in high esteem throughout Portugal, but nowhere more so than on the Costa Azul. The silver scabbard is less common than it used to be, fetching increasingly high prices, and local fishermen have been forced to sail further from shore to fish the black scabbard fish, more plentiful but not so highly rated.

Maria Jose's favourite recipe for either sort is this one, where it is partnered with lots of fresh green peas. It is a spring recipe, best when the new peas are being picked from gardens, though she says that she often makes it with frozen peas at other times of the year.

SERVES 4

3 cloves garlic, chopped
4 fl oz (120 ml) olive oil
3 onions, chopped
1½ lb (750 g) peas (shelled weight),
    thawed if frozen
4 tablespoons *passata*
salt and pepper

2 tablespoons finely chopped fresh parsley
3 fl oz (85 ml) white wine
4 chunks of scabbard fish or conger eel
    weighing about 1½–2 lb (750–
    900 g) in total
2 tablespoons chopped fresh coriander

Put the garlic and oil into a large pan and set over a medium heat. Stir until the garlic is just beginning to colour, then add the onions. Cook over a low–medium heat, stirring occasionally, until the onion is translucent, without browning. Now add the peas, *passata*, 4 fl oz (120 ml) water and salt and pepper. Simmer together for about 20 minutes, stirring occasionally. Stir in the parsley.

Transfer to a wide flameproof dish. Rinse out the pan with the wine and pour over the peas. Lay the slices of fish on top and return to the stove. Bring to a very gentle simmer, cover and cook for 10–15 minutes, turning the slices of fish once, until they are cooked through. Sprinkle with coriander and serve.

OVERLEAF
Background: *Peixe Espada com Ervilhas* (Scabbard Fish with Peas) see p.45.
Foreground: *Arroz de Mariscos* (Seafood Rice) see p.48.

Arroz de Mariscos
Seafood Rice

Though this is similar to a seafood paella, it isn't the same by any means. It turns out fairly soupy, or at least it should, with the rice soaking in a rich tomato broth, mussels, clams and prawns nestled on top. And where a paella is, or at least should be, fragrant with saffron, Arroz de Mariscos is characteristically Portuguese with a good dose of fresh green coriander.

SERVES 4–6

1 lb (450 g) mussels
1 lb (450 g) small clams
4 tablespoons olive oil
1 onion, chopped
2 cloves garlic, chopped
12 oz (350 g) tomatoes, skinned, seeded
   and chopped
1 tablespoon tomato purée

1 bay leaf
1 sprig of fresh parsley
1 dried red chilli
12 oz (350 g) long grain rice
salt and pepper
1 lb (450 g) raw prawns in their shells
2 tablespoons chopped fresh coriander

Scrub the mussels well, scraping off the beards and barnacles. Rinse thoroughly in several changes of water and discard any that stay open when tapped sharply against a work surface. Rinse the clams thoroughly in several changes of water. Pour a 1-inch (2.5-cm) depth of water into a large pan and bring to the boil. Add the mussels, cover and shake over a high heat until opened. Discard any that steadfastly refuse to open. Repeat with the clams. Pour the cooking liquid into a bowl and leave to settle, then pour off carefully, leaving any grit behind. Reserve. Shell half the clams and mussels, discarding the shells.

Put the oil, onion and garlic into a wide pan and cook over a medium heat until the onion is tender. Now add the tomatoes, tomato purée, bay leaf, parsley and chilli and cook for a further 5–10 minutes until thick. Add the rice, the cooking water from the mussels and clams, 1½ pints (900 ml) water, salt and pepper. Bring to the boil and simmer until the rice is tender and the mixture is soupy (if it seems dry, add a splash or two of boiling water). Lay the prawns in the mixture and cook for a few minutes more until they are done. Finally add both the shelled and unshelled mussels and clams, and the coriander, and heat through thoroughly. Taste and adjust the seasoning, then serve.

Porco à Alentejana
Pork with Clams

Though this dish comes from the Alentejo, which borders on the Costa Azul, it is now made all over Portugal,and you are just as likely to come across it in somewhere like Sesimbra as in its nearby home territory.

The combination of pork and clams appears an unpromising match at first glance, but it is one that is surprisingly successful. The sweetness of the shellfish is a natural enhancer of the meatiness of the braised pork. If you can't get small clams, mussels can be used instead, but you'll have to clean them immaculately, rinsing in three or four changes of water to get rid of as much grit as possible.

SERVES 4–6

1½ lb (750 g) pork (shoulder, loin or boneless chops), cut into 1-inch (2.5-cm) dice
1 heaped teaspoon paprika
10 fl oz (300 ml) dry white wine
3–4 cloves garlic, chopped
salt and pepper

1½ lb (750 g) small clams or mussels
1 oz (25 g) lard
2 tablespoons olive oil
1 onion, chopped
2 tablespoons chopped fresh parsley
1 tablespoon tomato purée
2 tablespoons chopped fresh coriander

Marinate the pork for at least 1 hour (4 or 5 hours is better) with the paprika, wine, half the garlic, salt and pepper. Meanwhile scrub the clams well, rinse in several changes of water, and discard any that remain open when tapped sharply on a work surface. Keep cool until needed.

Take the meat out of the marinade and pat dry on kitchen paper. Reserve the marinade. Brown the pork, in 2 batches, in the lard and olive oil over a brisk heat. Remove from the pan and set aside. Reduce the heat and add the onion, remaining garlic and parsley to the fat and cook gently until tender. Return the pork to the pan along with the marinade and tomato purée. Bring to a simmer, then cover and cook very gently for about 1 hour, until the pork is tender, checking occasionally. If necessary, add a little more wine or water. By the time the pork is done, the sauce should be reduced by about half.

Raise the heat and add the clams and coriander. Cover tightly and shake over a high heat for 2–3 minutes, until the clams have opened (discard any that stay closed). Draw off the heat, taste and adjust the seasoning, and serve.

Ⓥ
Pudim Molotov
Light-as-air Pudding

Portuguese puddings major heavily on the use of egg yolks, which inevitably means an awful lot of unused whites sitting in bowls around the kitchen. This is one pudding that uses them up most dramatically and successfully. Pudim Molotov is a high-rise dome of delicate meringue, often laced with a drizzling of caramel, easier to make than it at first appears. Helpings always look quite over the top, but the pudim *is as light and airy as a cloud, and it's amazing how quickly it slips down.*

SERVES 6–8

12 oz (350 g) caster sugar
8 large egg whites
butter for greasing the mould

Butter a 3-pint (1.75-litre) ring mould or other metal mould.

Place 8 oz (225 g) of the sugar in a pan with 3 fl oz (85 ml) water. Stir over a medium heat until the sugar has completely dissolved. Brush down any crystals stuck to the side of the pan with a pastry brush dipped in cold water. Bring to the boil and stop stirring. Boil hard for approximately 5–10 minutes, until the sugar caramelizes. Watch over it, and remove from the heat as soon as it is a good rich brown but before it begins to burn. Wrap a tea-towel around your hand and gradually pour 3 fl oz (85 ml) water into the caramel – it may spit a little, hence the tea-towel. Swirl around to dissolve the caramel, warming again gently, and stirring to dissolve lumps if necessary. Spoon 3 tablespoons of the caramel syrup into the mould, tipping and tilting so that it covers the base.

Pre-heat the oven to 350°F (180°C), gas mark 4.

Keep the rest of the syrup warm while you whisk the egg whites until stiff. Add the remaining sugar and whisk until glossy. Quickly bring the syrup back to the boil and pour it slowly but steadily into the egg whites, whisking constantly (an electric hand-whisk is a great help here). Whisk for a further 30 seconds–1 minute, until thick. Pour into the mould, smoothing over the top. Stand in a roasting tin of hot water and bake in the oven for 15–20 minutes, until golden-brown and firm to the touch.

Let the pudding cool for a minute or so, ease the edges away gently from the mould with the blade of a knife, then invert on to a shallow serving dish. Remove the mould and leave the pudding to cool (it will sink a little, but don't worry). Serve at room temperature on its own or with a runny egg-yolk custard (see below) or cream. I often serve it with soft fruit and/or single cream, though this is not at all Portuguese.

Ⓥ
Ovos Moles
Syrup Custard

Ovos Moles is a type of custard, made with a sugar syrup rather than milk. It's sweet and sticky, often made very thick and served on its own. This thinner version is good as a sauce with a Pudim Molotov.

SERVES 6

6 oz (175 g) sugar
8 egg yolks, lightly beaten

Put the sugar and a generous 10 fl oz (300 ml) water into a pan and stir over a moderate heat until the sugar has dissolved. Bring to the boil and boil hard for 5 minutes. Draw off the heat, let the bubbles subside, then pour into the egg yolks, whisking constantly as you pour. Return the mixture to the pan and stir over a low heat until the mixture thickens to a runny custard. Don't let it get anywhere near boiling point or it will curdle.

For the more usual, thicker *Ovos Moles* use only 5 fl oz (150 ml) water. The final custard will be thick enough to stand the spoon up in.

Ⓥ

Fatias Reais
Sweet Egg Bread in Syrup

This way of using up old bread is wonderfully rich and eggy and decadent. The slices of bread are soaked in egg yolks, and then poached in a sugar syrup. I like them warm, just lightly dusted with cinnamon, though they usually seem to be served cold in Portugal with a few shreds of very sweet pumpkin preserve.

SERVES 4

6 egg yolks plus 1 egg white
12 oz (350 g) caster sugar
zest of ½ lemon, pared off in wide strips
1 tablespoon lemon juice

4 × ½-inch (1-cm)-thick slices of day-old
    bread, crusts removed
ground cinnamon
pumpkin jam (optional)

Beat the egg yolks with the white and strain into a shallow dish. Put the sugar and lemon zest into a pan with 5 fl oz (150 ml) water and stir over a moderate heat until the sugar has completely dissolved. Brush down any crystals clinging to the sides of the pan with a brush dipped in cold water. Bring the syrup to the boil, stop stirring and boil until it reaches the thread stage – 234°F (112°C). Use a sugar thermometer as a guide, if you have one, but double-check manually: dip a pair of spoons back to back into the syrup, withdraw them and gently pull apart – if threads of sugar form between the spoons, you are there. Draw off the heat and stir in the lemon juice. Pour the syrup into a wide frying-pan.

Now for the real action. Heat the syrup until just simmering. Dip the slices of bread, 2 at a time, into the egg-yolk mixture, coating them thoroughly. Pop into the syrup and cook for 1 minute on each side. Lay the slices on a serving dish and sprinkle with cinnamon. Serve warm or cold, garnished with threads of pumpkin jam if you have any.

Ⓥ

Arroz Doce
Portuguese Rice Pudding

Arroz Doce, always eaten cold, is to be found on the menu of almost every café and small restaurant in Portugal – at least, in my limited experience. When made well, with good ingredients, as it is at Maria-Jose's café, it is one of the nicest rice puddings imaginable. The rice is cooked first in water to soften it, then again in milk to make it meltingly tender. Butter and egg yolks render it rich and velvety.

7 oz (200 g) medium-grain rice	zest of 1 lemon, pared off in strips
salt	6 oz (175 g) caster sugar
generous 1 pint (600 ml) creamy milk	8 egg yolks
3½ oz (90 g) butter	ground cinnamon

Boil the rice in plenty of water with a pinch of salt, until barely tender. Drain thoroughly and place in a large pan with the milk, butter and lemon zest. Bring to the boil and simmer for about 20 minutes until thick and creamy. Draw off the heat and stir in the sugar and then the egg yolks. Divide between 6–8 bowls, dust generously with ground cinnamon and leave to cool.

Ⓥ

Pêssegos Herdade de Zambujal
Baked Peaches in Wine

The Herdade de Zambujal is a huge peach-growing (and bull-raising) estate three-quarters of an hour's drive down the coast from Sesimbra. Right through the height of the peach season, there's always a dish of these baked peaches waiting to be eaten in the kitchen of the grand family house. Their eighty-year-old cook usually uses white wine, but occasionally substitutes a fruity red.

SERVES 6

6 peaches, skinned but whole
4 oz (100 g) caster sugar
1 cinnamon stick
½–¾ bottle dry white or red wine
ground cinnamon

Pre-heat the oven to 350°F (180°C), gas mark 4.

Place the peaches in a close-fitting ovenproof dish. Dredge with the sugar and tuck the cinnamon stick down among them. Pour over enough wine almost to cover. Bake in the oven until tender – about 40–50 minutes, depending on their ripeness and size – turning them once or twice, then leave to cool. Just before serving, dust lightly with cinnamon.

Ⓥ
Pastéis de Nata
Custard Tarts

Pastéis de Nata are not quite like ordinary custard tarts. For a start the custard is rich and tender, made usually with egg yolks rather than whole eggs. And then there's the pastry, a puff pastry, but rolled out in a most unusual way, so that the pastry case is a mass of fine overlapping layers. The instructions may sound a little confusing, but follow them step by step and you'll soon understand how they work.

MAKES 14

8 oz (225 g) puff pastry

Filling

4 egg yolks
2 oz (50 g) caster sugar
2 teaspoons flour
7 fl oz (200 ml) single cream

To serve

ground cinnamon
icing sugar

Roll out the pastry thinly into a rectangle 14 × 8 inches (35 × 20 cm). Roll up tightly from one of the short edges to form a plump sausage shape 8 inches (20 cm) long. Wrap in foil and chill in the freezer until firm but not frozen solid. Using a sharp knife, cut into discs ½ inch (1 cm) thick. Using your fingers, press each circle into a deep tartlet tin, easing the pastry up the sides. Prick with a fork and rest for 30 minutes in the refrigerator.

Pre-heat the oven to 450°F (230°C), gas mark 8.

Beat the egg yolks with the sugar and the flour. Gradually beat in the cream. Pour into a pan and stir over a gentle heat, without boiling, until you have a thick custard. Cool. Fill the tartlets two-thirds full with custard. Bake in the oven for 10–15 minutes, until the custard has browned. Eat warm or cold, dusted with cinnamon and icing sugar.

Gascony
FRANCE

Soups and Starters
Tourin d'Ivrogne Leek and Garlic Soup   p.60
Terrine de Foie Gras Baked Foie Gras   p.60
Foie Gras aux Raisins Foie Gras with Grapes   p.62
Foie Gras aux Figues Foie Gras with Figs   p.62
Fritons Duck or Goose 'Crackling'   p.69

Main Courses
Palombes Palombières Wood Pigeon Hunter-style   p.63
Lapin aux Pruneaux d'Agen Rabbit with Prunes   p.64
Magret de Canard au Confit d'Oignons Grilled Duck Breast with
    Caramelized Onion   p.65
Confit de Canard Duck *Confit*   p.68
La Poule-au-pot de Mme Fouteau Mme Fouteau's Chicken in a Pot   p.70

Vegetables
Cèpes à la Grille Grilled Ceps   p.72
Cèpes à la Persillade Ceps with Garlic and Parsley   p.73
Salade aux Endives et aux Noix Chicory and Walnut Salad   p.74

Desserts
Glace à l'Armagnac et aux Pruneaux Prune and Armagnac Ice-cream   p.75
Croustade aux Pommes Apple and Armagnac Filo Tart   p.76
Croustade aux Pruneaux et aux Pommes Apple and Prune Pie   p.78

Preserves and Biscuits
Confiture de Figues Fig Jam   p.79
Gelée de Coings Quince Jelly   p.80

Gascony
FRANCE

The ancient province of Gascony in the south-west of France does not officially exist any longer, but the French cleave tight to their old traditions. Locals are in no doubt that they are Gascons first and foremost, not merely inhabitants of the modern *départements* of the Gers, or those other new-fangled creations that impinge on their territory. They are proud of their heritage and of their land, of their most famous son, Charles de Batz, otherwise known as the musketeer D'Artagnan, and above all of their gastronomy.

This is the home of two of France's most luxurious products, Armagnac and *foie gras*, the liver of fattened ducks or geese. We'd set off in search of these two indulgences, but discovered much, much more in their shadow.

A chance introduction took us to the home of the Fouteau family, who are licensed to distil Armagnac from the juice of their grapes. These days licences are hard to come by and jealously guarded. October is a busy period – the *vendange* (grape harvest) is in full swing and the band of pickers, family, friends and a handful of employees are out, weather permitting, from early morning until twilight, pausing only in the middle of the day for a sustaining lunch.

Lunch and indeed the kitchen in general is Grandma Fouteau's business, and has been for the last half-century, since she came here as a young bride. Her territory extends outside to the small garden where she grows enough vegetables to keep the family fed, to the ducks on the pond, and to the chicken run, where she raises firm-fleshed free-range birds. Mémé Laure, as she is known to family and close friends, cooks as she has always done, using her own home-grown produce for dishes that she learnt from her mother.

Good food is important to all the family and, as with so many French people, their conversation comes around, again and again, to the subject. Every now and then a recipe is verbally dropped into my lap; have I ever tasted *Tourin d'Ivrogne*, drunkard's soup, made with leeks and garlic? No, but that was soon remedied.

Paulette and Jean-Pierre Picot run a *conserverie*, a small factory tinning and bottling *foie gras* and *confits*. Bizarrely they used to run a pub in central London, but

Foie Gras

A goose is a greedy bird, and has a tendency to gorge itself with as much food as it can lay its beak on just before it migrates. This eminently sensible behaviour has in one sense been its downfall, for long ago someone noticed that its liver was exceptionally tasty. It wasn't long before geese were being fattened up by man. The Romans, arch adapters as they were, used to feed their geese on sweet succulent figs, and seem to have borrowed the force-feeding idea from their Egyptian forebears. Today the French have inherited the mantle of bird stuffers *par excellence.*

Foie gras, which literally means 'fat liver', comes from geese or ducks that mostly lead a relatively uneventful life. For their last few weeks they are brought inside and force-fed three times a day with maize. In the right hands the process doesn't appear to be too brutal; the birds don't seem at all distressed and become somewhat stupefied by this permanent over-indulgence. The birds are, however, generally well treated and far happier than the average battery hen, though to many people the whole thing is still a ghastly idea. But it is a complex issue which requires careful thought.

The south-west of France, especially Gascony, has many small farms that make a living from *foie gras* – and the French countryside, let's face it, desperately needs as much income as possible from the land. In today's Europe, profit and loss rule the roost.

You will never be able to understand quite what the French feel about *foie gras* until you have actually tasted some. I am, I have to admit, a bit of a purist about food, and firmly believe that the best way to appreciate anything edible is in its simplest form. And so with *foie gras*. Start by eating it cold, *mi-cuit* or as a slice of terrine, a dish that is little more than the liver itself, seasoned, cooked and left to cool. To be sure, there are some exquisite recipes, but there is in my book nothing to rival the luscious simplicity of a slice of cold *foie gras*, to be savoured with toasted French country bread and perhaps a glass of Jurançon. To enjoy the very best, don't bother with any tins or jars unless they are clearly marked '100 per cent *foie gras*'. And try to make sure that the livers are French in origin. If there's a choice between goose or duck, go for the latter, which has the added bonus of being cheaper. Beware of those little tins of *parfait* and *pâtés*. They are invariably mixed with pork and taste quite horrible.

A plum-grower near Agen.

after ten years the lure of Paulette's native Gascony brought them back to the village of Lavardens.

Paulette's mother, Jeanette Espiau, is the real expert when it comes to *confits*. In the old days she reared *foie gras* geese herself on a small scale. Most of them were sold at market, but a dozen or so were kept for the family to sustain them through the winter, when they would eat *confits* two or three times a week.

Jean-Pierre took William off to the weekly *marché à gras* at Fleurance. This is where local farmers bring their fattened geese and ducks to be sold, strung together in braces, packed into the backs of cars, cackling and quacking in a veritable maelstrom of noise. There's an auction of chickens and a special market for eggs too. A whole hive of poultry-led activity spills over into the lower squares of the town.

Fleurance, like many of the small towns and villages round here, is a fortified *bastide*, built on a hill in the thirteenth century around an arcaded central market square, with grids of streets splaying outwards. The main food market floods down a street just off the main square and is packed with marvellous autumnal produce.

There are chestnuts and bulbous orange pumpkins, trays of wild mushrooms, sweet-scented chasselas and muscat grapes, golden and russet apples and quinces, figs and the pearly-white *crosnes*, Chinese artichoke – strange vegetables with a delicate flavour that lies somewhere between salsify and Jerusalem artichoke. The sight of a pile of Pyrenean cheeses, and then a Spanish *traiteur* selling chorizo, olive oil and ready-made paella, are reminders that we are little more than a couple of hours' drive from the border with Spain.

October is the prime hunting season, and wherever we drive we glimpse men, alone or in pairs, striding across the stubble of the wheat-fields, guns slung on their shoulders, faithful dogs sniffing and rootling around nearby. Rabbit is probably the main catch, though if they're lucky they may bag a pheasant or a hare; however, the real point of the exercise is not the catch at all but a day out in the open air.

This seems to be particularly true of the groups of five or six men who band together to hunt *palombes* (wild pigeons). We visited one *palombière* in a small wood set back off the main road from Condom to Auch. A *palombière* is a complicated set-up, and the first sign of it is a notice instructing the visitor to keep quiet and whistle for attention. As you attempt to whistle, you notice an odd network of wires strung from tree to tree and glimpse a doorway, masked with moss, set back among the trunks. This is the entrance to the long camouflaged corridor that leads down to the ramshackle 'control tower', where the men spend the entire day waiting for a flock of pigeons to fly over their wood.

The wires all begin here, and they lead off to strategically placed live decoy pigeons firmly laced to articulated metal perches high up among the leaves. As soon as the head hunter spies a flock of pigeons, he tugs at the wires, forcing the decoys to flap their wings and attract the attention of their wild cousins. The *palombes*, so the theory goes, are tricked into thinking that there is plentiful food to be had and make straight for the tree tops. Boom, boom, boom go the guns in the control tower and their fate is sealed. Mind you, it is unlikely that more than half a dozen birds at most are taken – a quick escape is easy through all the foliage.

If the thought of hunting upsets you, you may take some consolation in the fact that a hit is rare. Most days the men return home empty-handed, without even having glimpsed any wild pigeons, let alone taken a shot.

Ⓥ
Tourin d'Ivrogne
Leek and Garlic Soup

Translated literally, the name means 'drunkard's soup', though quite why I haven't the faintest idea. It is certainly soothing though it doesn't reek as highly of garlic as one might imagine. Made with those vegetables that a French farm worker might well have growing in his garden, plus stale bread, eggs from the hens and a flash of vinegar, it was a thrifty, nutritious and filling dish for those days when meat was too expensive even to contemplate.

SERVES 4–6

1 generous tablespoon duck or goose fat, or butter	1½ pints (900 ml) light stock or water
1 large onion, chopped	salt and pepper
6 cloves garlic, sliced	4 eggs
4 large leeks (white part only), sliced	3 tablespoons white wine vinegar
	4 slices stale bread, lightly toasted

Melt the fat in a large saucepan and add the onion, garlic and leeks. Stir, then cover and sweat over a low heat for 10 minutes. Add the stock or water, salt and pepper and bring to the boil. Simmer for 20 minutes. Carefully break the eggs and let the whites slide into the water, reserving the yolks. Do this one by one, directly over the pan. Poach gently for 5–10 minutes.

Beat the egg yolks with the vinegar and gradually stir in 5 tablespoons of the soup liquid. Once the egg whites are done, draw the soup off the heat and let the bubbles subside. Stir in the egg-yolk mixture, then taste and adjust the seasoning. Place a slice of bread in each soup bowl and ladle over the hot soup. Serve immediately.

Terrine de Foie Gras
Baked Foie Gras

Montréal is a classic small bastide *town, its old central square lined with arcaded walkways. Hidden discreetly behind the square is the deceptively simple-looking restaurant, Chez Simone. William and I treated ourselves to an epically good lunch here, which began with a terrine of* foie gras. *The waiter brought out an enormous dish packed to the gills with hummocks of fawn-pink* foie gras *sealed in its own yellow fat, from which he carved us long thick slices: totally over the top, and quite stunning. By the time we left the table, I felt so mellow that I barely noticed the enormity of the bill.*

Preparing *foie gras*

If you are lucky enough to be stranded with a whole *foie gras*, absolutely fresh or vacuum-packed, here's how to prepare it.

Soak the liver in a bowl of salted water for 2–3 hours. This dissolves and draws out the blood. Drain and, as best you can, pull off what you can find of the almost impossibly thin membrane wrapped around it. Gently ease the two lobes of *foie gras* apart. With the tip of a knife or a cloth, scrape or wipe away any greenish patches that are lurking (traces of the gall bladder, and ruinously bitter). Scrape away the veins and connective tissue between the lobes. Don't get too carried away on excavation work. It's important to remove the bigger veins, but if you dig around too much you'll end up with a mess of a liver.

Now the liver is ready to slice and flash-fry, or to bake *en terrine*, the simplest and perhaps the best way to deal with it.

Quantity

1¾–2 oz (40–50 g) *foie gras* per person is the usual restaurant portion, but anyone who likes it may well get through more. It all rather depends on what you can afford and how generous you're feeling.

1 (or more) prepared *foie gras* (see above)
½ tablespoon Armagnac or brandy to each
1 lb (450 g) *foie gras*
salt and pepper

Pre-heat the oven to 325°F (160°C), gas mark 3.

Rub about half the Armagnac into the *foie gras* and season all over with salt and pepper. Find a terrine or other deep ovenproof dish that will just take your *foie gras* snugly. Sprinkle a little of the remaining Armagnac in the base, ease the *foie gras* tightly into the terrine and sprinkle over the remaining Armagnac. Cover with foil.

Stand the terrine in a roasting tin and pour enough boiling water around the terrine to come about 1 inch (2.5 cm) up the sides. Bake in the oven for 30 minutes. Check occasionally and make sure that the water around the terrine is never boiling – if necessary, reduce the heat slightly. As the liver cooks and some of its fat oozes out, it will shrink. It can be rather disconcerting to see your erstwhile glory of a liver reduced to a shadow of its former self, but that's just life. The fat is delicious anyway – what doesn't get eaten with the terrine can be used instead of butter to sauté potatoes, among other things.

Cool the terrine until tepid, then cover with clean foil and weigh down with tins or other weights. Leave overnight in the refrigerator. Eat with hot toasted brioche or other good bread.

Foie Gras aux Raisins
Foie Gras with Grapes

I love hot foie gras, *but it's not the kind of thing that I often cook at home. Hardly ever, in fact. From my limited experience, however, I can tell you that the secret is to get the pan terrifyingly hot and to cook the slices of* foie gras *for the minimal time so that they don't melt away entirely. Even if you don't go on to make a sauce, whip the cooked* foie gras *straight on to pieces of toast, which will sop up the juice.*

The sweet freshness of grapes or figs, both fruit that grow abundantly in this area, is an ideal partner to the richness of the foie gras.

SERVES 4

4 × 1½-inch (1-cm)-thick slices prepared duck *foie gras* (see page 61) weighing 1¾–2 oz (45–50 g) each
4 slices toasted brioche or French bread
salt and pepper

7 fl oz (200 ml) sweet muscat wine
6 oz (175 g) white or black grapes, peeled and seeded if necessary
1 oz (25 g) butter, diced

Heat a heavy non-stick frying-pan until searingly hot. Lay the slices of *foie gras* in the pan, cook for about 30 seconds on each side – long enough to brown, but little more – then lay quickly on the slices of toasted bread and season with salt and pepper. Keep warm.

Pour the excess fat out of the pan and pour in the wine. Boil hard until reduced by half. Add the grapes, stir and let it bubble for a few seconds, then dot in the butter. Swirl and tilt the pan so that the butter melts into the sauce, enriching it without forming an oil-slick. Season and pour over the *foie gras*, then serve instantly.

Foie Gras aux Figues
Foie Gras with Figs

Cook the *foie gras* as in the above recipe, replacing the grapes with 4 ripe purple figs, quartered and briefly heated in the wine reduction.

Palombes Palombières
Wood Pigeon Hunter-style

Just because the likelihood of bagging a good haul of wild pigeons is minimal, doesn't mean that the hunters do without. It's not unheard of for them to buy a few wood pigeons, ready plucked for the pan, and bring them along for lunch! This is how they cook them in the smoky lower room of their control tower.

The recipe is simple enough to cook over a small two-ring camping-stove, but extremely effective. One wood pigeon makes a more than generous portion for one person, but if there are plenty of other things to eat, it'll feed two without meanness.

SERVES 4–8

olive oil
4 wood pigeons, cleaned
4 cloves garlic, roughly crushed
2 sprigs of fresh thyme (optional)
salt and pepper
2 tablespoons Armagnac or brandy

Cover the base of a heavy pan, large enough to take the 4 pigeons in a single layer, with a little olive oil. Heat over a medium heat and brown the pigeons briskly. Turn the pigeons breast side down, add the garlic, thyme (if using), salt and pepper and reduce the heat. In a separate pan gently warm the Armagnac. Set it alight at arm's length and pour over the pigeons. Once the flames have died down, cover the pan tightly and reduce the heat to low. Stew the pigeons in their own juices for about 1 hour, until tender. Check occasionally. With a well-fitting lid there should be no need to add water, but if the birds do threaten to burn, add a couple of tablespoons at most.

Lapin aux Pruneaux d'Agen
Rabbit with Prunes

We were only an hour or so's drive from Agen, home of the best prunes in the world, so I insisted on a day trip to visit a prune-producer. Lunch at the Gautiers was, as you might expect, based around their own juicy, new season's prunes, beginning with this delicious dish of rabbit. Eau-de-vie de prunes is a superb local spirit, scented with plums, which intensified the flavour of prunes, both in this main course and in the pie which followed (see p.78), but brandy works well as a substitute.

SERVES 4

1 lb (450 g) prunes (weighed with their stones)
2 fl oz (50 ml) *eau-de-vie de prunes* or brandy
6 oz (175 g) lardons or whole piece of smoked streaky bacon
2 tablespoons sunflower or groundnut oil
1 oz (25 g) unsalted butter
1 rabbit, cut into 8 pieces

4 shallots, chopped
1 heaped tablespoon flour
5 fl oz (150 ml) dry white wine
1 bouquet garni (1 bay leaf, 2 sprigs each of fresh thyme and parsley, tied together)
salt and pepper
parsley to garnish

Put the prunes to soak with the *eau-de-vie* and 3 fl oz (85 ml) water. Leave for 2 hours (or longer), turning occasionally. If using a whole piece of bacon, cut into thick batons about ½ inch (1 cm) in width and 1 inch (2.5 cm) long.

Heat the oil with the butter over a fairly high heat and brown the rabbit pieces briskly in 2 batches. Transfer to a heatproof casserole. Cook the shallots and lardons or bacon in the same fat over a moderate heat, until tender and translucent. Spoon around the rabbit, and sprinkle over the flour. Pour the excess fat out of the frying-pan, then add the wine and bring to the boil, stirring and scraping up the residues from frying. Pour over the rabbit, and tuck the bouquet garni in amongst the meat. Season with salt and pepper. Cover and simmer gently over a low heat for 1 hour. Turn the pieces of rabbit occasionally so that they cook evenly.

Now add the prunes and their soaking liquid, and simmer for a further 30 minutes, covered, until the rabbit is very tender.

To serve, arrange the pieces of rabbit in a shallow dish and surround with the prunes. Spoon a little of the pan juices over the meat and prunes to moisten, then cover and keep warm. Skim the fat off the rest, taste and adjust the seasoning. Strain into a sauce boat or jug and serve with the rabbit and prunes, garnished with a few sprigs of parsley or a scattering of chopped parsley.

Magret de Canard au Confit d'Oignons
Grilled Duck Breast with Caramelized Onion

Strictly speaking, magrets (or maigrets, *like the detective) are the breasts of* foie gras *ducks, but the word is now used for any duck breasts, as long as they are nice and plump. They are quick to grill and should remain pink at heart: never overcook to a uniform greyness through and through.*

The confit d'oignons *can be made well ahead of time and is good with any rich meat, be it duck, goose or pork. Served with the duck breasts, and a peppery rocket or watercress salad, it makes for a speedy chic dinner dish.*

SERVES 4

4 duck breasts
salt and pepper
sunflower or groundnut oil

Onion confit

1 oz (25 g) butter
1 tablespoon sunflower or groundnut oil
2 lb (900 g) onions, thinly sliced
2 oz (50 g) caster sugar

2 tablespoons red wine vinegar
2 teaspoons fresh thyme leaves
coarsely ground black pepper

The onion *confit* can be made several days in advance and stored in the refrigerator. Melt the butter with the oil in a wide pan and add the onions. Cook very gently, half-covered, over a low heat, stirring occasionally until the onions are golden and meltingly tender – about 40 minutes. Uncover and stir in the remaining ingredients. Continue cooking for a further 20 minutes or so, stirring frequently, until thick and jammy. Re-heat gently when needed.

Pre-heat the grill thoroughly. Rub salt and pepper into the skin of the duck breasts and grill, skin side to the heat, until well browned. Turn over, brush with oil and grill for a further 5–10 minutes, depending on how well you like them done and how plump the breasts are. Season with salt and pepper, turn off the grill and let the breasts rest for 5 minutes. Slice and arrange on serving plates with a dollop of the warmed onion *confit*.

OVERLEAF
Left: *Croustade aux Pommes* (Apple and Armagnac Filo Tart) see p.76.
Right: *Confiture de Figues* (Fig Jam) see p.79. Front: *Magret de Canard au Confit d'Oignons* (Grilled Duck Breast with Caramelized Onion) see p.65.

Confit de Canard
Duck *Confit*

We bought a beautiful, knee-length, yellow-glazed, earthenware pot à graisse *in Condom, which we then had to lug back on the plane. It is the kind of urn-shaped pot that would once have been found in every farmhouse in the region, filled to the brim with duck or goose fat and* confits.

Real confits *are made with* foie gras *birds, whose bodies are sheathed in thick layers of fat, more than enough to submerge the meat as it cooks. You can't get the real McCoy at the supermarket in Britain, or even the classiest of butchers, so if you want to make* confits *you'll have to boost the fat level by adding tinned duck or goose fat if you can find it or – less choice – lard.*

As long as the meat is completely covered with fat, it will keep for as long as a year in the refrigerator, though, you'll probably find that it doesn't get a chance to linger that long. The fat can be recycled for a second batch, or used to sauté potatoes or to flavour any number of other dishes.

SERVES 6 – 8

2 ducks
12 oz (350 g) coarse sea salt
2 oz (50 g) coarsely ground pepper
    (optional)
about 8 oz – 1 lb (225 – 450 g) extra duck
    or goose fat, or lard

Dismember the ducks: cut off the necks, legs and wings (snip off the bony tips and use for stock making), then remove the wishbone. Cut off the breasts – these can be put in with the *confit*, but they are best grilled or roasted fresh (see the recipe for *Magret de Canard* on p.65). Now examine the carcase and cut it up, adding the bits with meat on them to the *confit* pile. Bare bones should be saved for making stock. Carefully trim off all the knobs of fat, and stray folds of skin and reserve.

Mix the salt and pepper (if using) and rub into the chunks of meat that are to be made into *confit*. Place in a bowl and sprinkle any left-over salt over them. Cover with a tea-towel and leave in the refrigerator or a cool place for 12 hours.

Cut the reserved skin and fat into tiny pieces and place in a pan with a glass of water. Cook over a very low heat for about 1–1½ hours, until the fat has melted down. Strain and reserve the liquid fat. Keep the little bits for making *Fritons* (see below).

Next day, rinse all the salt and pepper thoroughly from the duck meat in a couple of changes of cold water. Dry carefully. Put the reserved fat and the extra fat into a heavy pan and warm over a very low heat. Add the pieces of duck. They must all be totally submerged in the fat, so you may not be able to get them all in in one go. Cook extremely gently for 1–1½ hours, without letting the fat boil, until the meat is very tender. You may need to use a diffuser mat to spread the heat more evenly, particularly towards the end of the cooking time. Skim off any scum that rises to the top.

Lift the cooked duck out and pack into a wide-mouthed earthenware jar. Cook the remaining pieces of duck in the same fat, in the same way, skimming regularly. When they are done, add these to the rest of the meat and pour over enough fat to cover completely. Leave overnight to cool and settle, then cover with greaseproof paper and tie it in place. Store the *confit* in the refrigerator, where it will keep for up to a year.

To use, extract pieces of meat and scrape off the excess fat. Fry or roast in the oven, pre-heated to 425°F (220°C), gas mark 7, until the skin is crisp and the meat is heated through. Serve with a green salad, and perhaps some potatoes sautéed in the fat.

Fritons
Duck or Goose 'Crackling'

Fry the bits of skin from rendering the fat for *confit* in a pan, with no extra fat, until richly browned and crisp – this takes about 30 minutes. Drain on kitchen paper. Season with salt. Serve as a 'nibble' to go with drinks.

La Poule-au-pot de Mme Fouteau
Mme Fouteau's Chicken in a Pot

This is a stunning one-pot (but two-course) dish for a party, and not half as complicated as it appears at first glance. Before you begin, make sure that you have a big enough pan or cauldron to take all the vegetables and bones as well as the stuffed chicken. I can just about get them into my large preserving pan with an inch or two to spare! You will also need to arm yourself with a stout needle and thread and a thimble – even if you don't normally use one when you sew, it really does help here as your fingers tend to get slippery and sticky. The bird is best stuffed the evening before, then all you have to do on the feast day is throw everything in the pot and leave it to simmer steadily for 3 hours.

The meal begins with the broth, made more substantial by the addition of tapioca (my favourite, and not to be overlooked merely because of childhood prejudice) or pasta. Next comes the chicken with its stuffing, some of the vegetables from the broth for those who want them, and freshly boiled potatoes and cauliflower, moistened with a little of the chicken broth. At the Fouteau's they usually finish up with roast duck to fill any lingering gaps!

SERVES 6–8

1 large boiling hen

Stuffing

¼ onion, chopped	4 oz (100 g) best-quality minced beef
2 tablespoons chopped fresh parsley	2 oz (50 g) sausagemeat
3 cloves garlic, chopped	3 oz (75 g) soft white breadcrumbs
1 veal escalope weighing about 4½ oz (120 g), chopped	salt and pepper
chicken liver and gizzard, chopped	5 eggs

Broth

2 large onions, quartered	4 leeks, trimmed and tied together in a bundle
6 cloves garlic, peeled	½ Savoy cabbage, quartered
4 carrots	½ celeriac root, peeled
3 turnips, quartered	salt and pepper
2 lb (900 g) veal or beef bones	1½ pints (900 ml) *passata*
1 generous bouquet garni (2 bay leaves, 3 sprigs each of fresh thyme and parsley, tied together)	

For the soup

4 oz (100 g) tapioca or vermicelli

Begin by making the stuffing, which is easiest done in a processor. Put all the ingredients except the eggs in the processor and whizz until fairly smooth. Keep the motor running and break in the eggs one at a time, to make a fairly sloppy purée.

Thread your needle and sew up the wishbone end of the chicken tightly so that none of the stuffing can seep out. Prop the chicken firmly, open end upwards, in a small saucepan or bowl so that you can stuff it. With your fingers and a spoon, gently ease the skin away from the flesh on the breast, and spoon about one-quarter of the stuffing under the skin, smoothing it down so that it protects the meat. Fill the cavity with the rest.

Wash your hands and put a new piece of thread in the needle. Sew up the skin and hole really carefully and tightly. Remember that the stuffing is runny and you don't want it to leak out into the water, nor do you want any more liquid oozing in to dilute it before it is set. Truss the chicken tightly with string so that it doesn't fall apart in the pan. If you have time, leave the chicken overnight, loosely covered, in the refrigerator.

When you are ready to cook, take a huge pan, big enough to hold the chicken, vegetables and bones with plenty of room to spare. Half-fill with water, cover and bring to the boil – allow plenty of time. Now add all the broth ingredients except the *passata*, bring back to the boil and slip in the chicken. There should be enough water to cover everything by several inches. If necessary, add more boiling water. Skim off all the scum that rises to the surface. Simmer for 2 hours, then add the *passata*. Continue simmering for a further 1–2 hours, topping up with more boiling water as needed.

When you are about 30 minutes or so away from sitting down to eat, it's back to work. Hoick the chicken out carefully, cover and keep warm in the oven. Ladle about 3 pints (1.75 litres) of the cooking broth into a clean pan, bring to the boil and add the tapioca or vermicelli. Bring back to the boil, simmer for 5 minutes, then cover tightly and turn off the heat. Go back to the chicken, dismember it and arrange pieces on a serving plate together with slices of the stuffing. Spoon over a little broth to keep it all moist, cover with foil and keep warm in the oven.

I quite like the meltingly soft, long-boiled vegetable from the broth, and save up a plate of them, pappy as they are, for kindred spirits. On the other hand, if you feel they've more than served their purpose, which is to impart flavour to everything else, you are quite justified in throwing them straight into the bin.

Taste and adjust the seasoning in the soup and serve, then follow with chicken, stuffing, vegetables from the broth if using, and freshly cooked vegetables.

ⓥ
Cèpes à la Grille
Grilled Ceps

We took Mme Fouteau a present of some wild mushrooms, ceps, that we had bought in the market at Fleurance: a good move, as the local yield had been poor this year — these came from the foothills of the Pyrenees, which, on a clear day, can just be seen in the distance.

The whole family is passionate about ceps. Mme Fouteau told me that the year when she was pregnant with Joel was a particularly good one for wild mushrooms. A month or so before he was born she developed a ravenous passion for them, downing twenty-two at one meal, and that after half a roast chicken! No wonder he likes them so much.

We all sat down to prepare them together, Joel taking charge of the large ones which he grilled over the embers of the fire. The stalks and smaller ceps were handed over to his mother to cook.

> large ceps at least 3 inches (7.5 cm) across
> cloves garlic, cut into thin slivers
> sunflower or groundnut oil
> salt and pepper

Clean the ceps with a cloth, scraping off any leaves and other gunge with a knife. Cut out any wormy bits. Slice off the stems and save for some other dish (such as the *persillade* on p.73). With the tip of a sharp knife, make slits in the caps, and push slivers of garlic down into them. Quite how many depends on the size of the caps and your fondness for garlic, but don't be too stingy. Brush with oil, season with salt and pepper and grill gently, smooth side upwards at first, turning the spongy side up later, until tender. Allow a good 15–20 minutes, so that both the mushrooms and the garlic are cooked right through.

ⓥ
Cèpes à la Persillade
Ceps with Garlic and Parsley

This is how Mme Fouteau cooked the smaller caps in the batch. As with the preceding recipe, I've not specified quantities. Being precise seems a bit pointless – who can say how many you'll find if you pick your own, and who can say how many you'll be able to afford if you splash out on bought ceps, always phenomenally pricey. Use your imagination, and this outline as a guide, and you are unlikely to go wrong.

small–medium ceps less than 3 inches (7.5 cm) across
a few cloves garlic, cut into slivers
goose fat, or ½ butter and ½ sunflower or groundnut oil

finely chopped parsley
finely chopped garlic
a handful of fresh breadcrumbs
salt and pepper

Clean the ceps as described on p.72. Leave the caps whole; make 2 or 3 slits in each one and push in a sliver of garlic. Slice the stems thickly. Keep the caps and stems separate. Melt a generous amount of fat in two separate pans and put the caps in one, the stems in the other. Cook gently, stirring and turning every now and then, for a good 20 minutes or so, until they begin to colour.

Throw a small handful of chopped parsley and garlic in with the stems, and carry on cooking for 3–4 minutes. Now add just enough breadcrumbs to each pan to sop up a good deal of the fat, and then season with salt and pepper. Stir for 2 minutes or so, then serve piping hot.

Ⓥ
Salade aux Endives et aux Noix
Chicory and Walnut Salad

Chicory and walnuts are perfect bed-fellows. They make the best of autumn or winter salads, when other greenery is in short supply. Refreshing, and cleansing after a heavy, meaty main course.

SERVES 4

3 large heads of chicory
2 oz (50 g) walnut pieces

Dressing

½ tablespoon white wine vinegar
¼ teaspoon Dijon mustard
salt and pepper
2½ – 3 tablespoons groundnut or
  sunflower oil

Make the dressing in the salad bowl. Whisk the vinegar with the mustard, salt and pepper. Gradually beat in the oil, a tablespoon at a time. Taste and adjust the seasoning. Cross salad servers in the bowl.

  Cut the base off the chicory and discard along with any damaged outer leaves. Separate the heads into individual leaves and pile on top of the salad servers in the bowl. Scatter with walnuts. Toss just before eating.

Ⓥ
Glace à l'Armagnac et aux Pruneaux
Prune and Armagnac Ice-cream

If prunes suggest nursery food and childhood horrors, this ice-cream will redress the balance. It's strictly for grown-ups, and definitely for dinner parties rather than daily consumption. Soak the prunes for as long as you can, so that they have plenty of time to absorb the flavour of the Armagnac or brandy.

SERVES 6–8

5 oz (150 g) caster sugar
5 tablespoons Armagnac or brandy
1 lb (450 g) prunes (weighed with their
    stones)

10 fl oz (300 ml) milk
1 vanilla pod, slit open
4 egg yolks
10 fl oz (300 ml) double cream

Put 3 oz (75 g) of the sugar in a pan with 5 fl oz (150 ml) water. Stir over a moderate heat until dissolved. Bring to the boil, then draw off the heat. Stir in the Armagnac and pour over the prunes. Cover and leave to soak for at least 24 hours, if not 2 or 3 days, then pit the prunes and purée them with their syrup.

Bring the milk and vanilla pod to the boil. Cover and infuse over the lowest possible heat for 10 minutes, then remove the vanilla pod. Whisk the egg yolks lightly with the remaining sugar. Pour on the hot milk, stirring constantly. Set the bowl over a pan of lazily simmering water, making sure that the base does not touch the water. Stir until just thick enough to coat the back of a spoon. Draw off the heat and strain. Stir in the prune purée and cool. Whip the cream lightly and fold in the prune custard.

Freeze in a sorbetière if you have one. Otherwise pour into a shallow container and place in the freezer, set to its lowest setting. When half-set, beat hard to break up the crystals. Return to the freezer. Freeze until almost solid, then beat hard again (in a processor, if you like). Freeze until solid.

(V)

Croustade aux Pommes
Apple and Armagnac Filo Tart

Making a genuine croustade *is no easy feat – it takes considerable skill to stretch the dough out so very thin that you can read your watch through it. I have resorted to bought filo pastry for my* croustade. *It's not quite the same, but the results are still impressive. The sheets of filo that I used were fairly large, about 14 × 16 inches (35 × 40 cm). If yours are smaller, use two where I have folded mine in half. Choose apples that really are golden and ripe.*

SERVES 8

8 oz (225 g) granulated or caster sugar
5 fl oz (150 ml) Armagnac or brandy
1 teaspoon natural vanilla essence

2 lb (900 g) ripe Golden Delicious apples,
    peeled, cored and thinly sliced
4 oz (100 g) unsalted butter, melted
15 sheets filo pastry

The day before you intend to eat the *croustade*, make the Armagnac syrup. Put the sugar into a pan with 5 fl oz (150 ml) water, stir over a medium heat until the sugar has dissolved, then bring to the boil. Draw off the heat and stir in the Armagnac and vanilla essence. Leave to cool.

Peel and core the apples, then slice very thinly. Set aside 4 tablespoons of the syrup and pour the rest over the apples, turning the slices gently. Cover with a cloth and leave at room temperature overnight.

Next day, brush a 10-inch (25-cm) tart tin with butter. To prevent the filo pastry drying out as you work, pile up the sheets, cover with a sheet of greaseproof paper and lay a tea-towel wrung out in cold water over the paper. Put a metal baking sheet in the oven and pre-heat it to 400°F (200°C), gas mark 6.

Take the first sheet of filo, brush lightly with butter, fold in half and lay in the tin, one corner inwards, so that it covers about one-third of the base with the ends trailing over the side. Do the same with a second sheet, laying it at right angles to the first. Repeat with a further 6 sheets of filo (making 8 in all so far), gently pressing them down so that they line the tin. Take a 9th sheet, brush with butter and lay it over the entire base, without folding.

Now fill the tart with slices of apple, making sure that they lie flat. Spoon over 2–3 tablespoons of their soaking syrup. Flip the trailing ends of filo over to cover the filling, smoothing them down nicely, but still leaving an inch or so hanging over the edge. Brush another sheet of filo with butter, fold in half and lay it over the top. Trim off the edges close to the tin with a sharp knife or a pair of scissors.

Time for a bit of artistry. Taking a sheet of filo at a time (no need for butter here), scrunch it up gently in your hands, then lay it on top of the *croustade* so that it balloons up in crumpled waves, covering about one-fifth of the surface. Repeat with another 4 sheets, to finish with a casual-looking arrangement of elegantly scrumpled filo covering the entire *croustade*. Dip the brush in melted butter and flick it over the pastry. Don't try to brush on the butter or you'll flatten those chic waves.

Set the *croustade* on the hot baking sheet (this gives an instant blast of heat to the underside, so that it cooks more crisply) and bake for 15 minutes, then reduce the heat to 350°F (180°C), gas mark 4, and bake for a further 30 minutes (cover loosely with foil if it threatens to burn). As soon as it comes out of the oven, brush with the reserved Armagnac syrup. Work lightly so as not to crack the filo, but be generous and use it all up. Serve warm (it can be re-heated briefly in the oven).

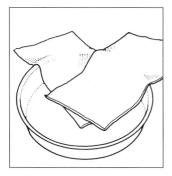

1 Take each sheet of filo pastry; brush with butter, fold in half, then lay one corner in the tin so it covers about a third of the base. Add each sheet in the same way at right angles to the one before it.

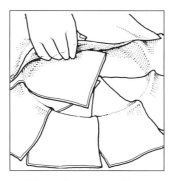

2 When all the sheets have been placed in the tin, press them down so they line the tin. Take another sheet of pastry and lay over the entire base without folding.

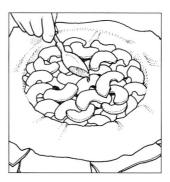

3 Fill the tart with slices of apple, making sure they lie down flat. Spoon over 2–3 tablespoons of their syrup.

4 Flip the trailing edges of the filo over to cover the filling, smoothing them down nicely. Leave 1 inch (2.5 cm) trailing over the edge of the tart tin.

5 Brush a piece of filo pastry with butter, fold it in half and lay it over the top of the tart. Trim off the edges close to the tin using a sharp knife or scissors.

6 Take one sheet of filo pastry at a time, scrunch it up gently in your hands then lay it on top of the *croustade* so it balloons up.

Ⓥ
Croustade aux Pruneaux et aux Pommes
Apple and Prune Pie

This croustade *was made for me by Martine Gautier, prune-grower, when we detoured up to Agen for the day. Only a little further north and the* croustade *changes character to become a puff-pastry pie, in this case filled with prunes and apples.*

SERVES 6–8

1¾ lb (785 g) puff pastry
3 ripe Golden Delicious apples, peeled, cored and thinly sliced
8 oz (225 g) prunes, soaked and then pitted

4 oz (100 g) vanilla sugar, or 4 oz (100 g) caster sugar and 1 teaspoon natural vanilla essence
3 tablespoons *eau-de-vie de prunes* or Armagnac or brandy

To glaze

1 egg yolk, lightly beaten
extra caster sugar

Put a baking sheet in the oven and preheat to 425°F (220°C), gas mark 7.

Roll out about two-thirds of the pastry and use to line a 10-inch (25-cm) loose-bottomed cake tin, 2–3 inches (5–7.5 cm) deep. Press it down gently into the corners and leave the excess hanging over the sides. Put the apple slices in the pie, then the stoned prunes, then sprinkle over the sugar, vanilla essence (if using) and the *eau-de-vie*. Brush the edges of the pastry with a little of the egg-yolk glaze.

Roll out the remaining pastry and place over the pie. Trim the edges nicely and press firmly together. Make a hole in the centre. Use the trimmings, if you wish, to cut out shapes to decorate the *croustade*, and glue them on with egg-yolk glaze. Rest in the refrigerator for 30 minutes if you have time.

Brush with egg-yolk glaze, sprinkle with caster sugar and set on the piping-hot baking sheet in the oven. After 15 minutes reduce the heat to 350°F (180°C), gas mark 4, and bake for a further 25 minutes. Cover loosely with foil if the top is browning too quickly. Cool for a few minutes in the tin, then unmould carefully. Serve hot or warm.

ⓥ
Confiture de Figues
Fig Jam

This jam was inspired by the breakfast jams of Mme Manet at the Hôtel des Trois Lys in Condom. A brush with Weight Watchers induced her to reduce the sugar content of her home-made jams, and they taste all the better for it. However, less sugar means that this jam won't reach a firm set, always remaining more runny than the usual British style of jam.

MAKES about 3½ lb (1.5 kg)

2 lb (900 g) purple or green figs, not too
    ripe
2 lemons
3 cloves
1 lb (450 g) granulated or caster sugar

Nip the hard stems off the figs, then quarter the fruit. Grate the zest of the lemons finely. Squeeze the juice, and reserve the pips. Tie the pips and the cloves in a square of muslin. Put the figs in a pan with the lemon juice, pips and 5 fl oz (150 ml) water. Bring gently to a simmer and simmer for 15 minutes until the figs are tender. Now add the sugar and lemon zest and stir until the sugar has completely dissolved. Bring back to the boil and boil until thick and syrupy – about 40 minutes.

Remove the muslin bag and let the jam settle for 5 minutes. Ladle into hot sterilized jam jars (see below), cover and seal as normal. Store in a cool dark place and use within 3 months. Store the jars, once opened, in the refrigerator.

To sterilize jars

Wash the jars in warm soapy water, then rinse in hot water. Without touching the insides, place them on a wire rack in the oven, set to 225°F (110°C), gas mark ¼. Leave for at least 30 minutes, until the jam is ready to be potted.

ⓥ
Gelée de Coings
Quince Jelly

One of my all-time favourite jellies, with its glowing amber colour and heavenly perfume. First, though, you must find your quinces. I'm lucky in that I have a Greek greengrocer down the road who imports them from Cyprus every autumn. If you don't grow any yourself, it's worth asking around to see if any neighbours have a tree hidden away in their garden. With luck you will be able to scrounge a few windfalls (but do be careful to remove all blemishes and bruises before using the quinces), and if necessary you can eke them out by adding a couple of cooking apples.

quinces
granulated sugar

Wash the quinces and rub off the fine fluff. Cut out and discard any blemished or bruised patches. Chop up the rest of the quinces, peel, core and all, and throw into a large heavy pan, adding enough water to come about half-way up the fruit. Bring to the boil and boil hard until the fruit is very tender and pulpy. Stir, and mush down occasionally as it cooks.

Tip the contents of the pan into a jelly bag, or a non-metallic sieve lined with a double layer of muslin, and let the juice drip through. Don't press down on the pulp or you'll end up with a cloudy jelly. Leave it to drip into a bowl for at least 2 hours, or overnight if possible.

Measure the quantity of juice, and for each pint (600 ml) weigh out 1 lb (450 g) sugar. Stir together, in a clean pan, over a moderate heat until the sugar has dissolved. Bring to the boil and boil hard until setting point is reached. Ladle into hot sterilized jars (see p.79), seal and label.

To test for setting point

If you have one, use a sugar thermometer as a guide to setting point, but don't rely on it absolutely. Always back it up by testing manually; drip a drop of the jam on to a chilled saucer. Cool for a few minutes, then nudge with your finger nail. If the surface wrinkles, the jam is ready; if it doesn't, repeat a few minutes later.

Sicily
ITALY

First Courses and Anti-pasti

Pasta

Main Courses

Desserts

Preserves

Sicily
ITALY

There's no better introduction to the foods of Sicily than a visit to one of the teeming markets of Palermo. Il Ballarò is not the biggest – that honour goes to La Vucceria – but it is every bit as energetic, fascinating and noisy as you would expect of a southern market. Stalls and shoppers and, we were warned, pickpockets crowd into the narrow over-hanging back streets that broaden out here and there into small squares allowing a glimpse of the green-tiled dome of the neighbourhood church. Splashes of sunshine force their way down between the high tenement buildings, highlighting mountains of blood-red cherries or a tangled skein of intestines on a butcher's slab.

The poverty and decay of the area is disguised by the sheer exuberance of the scene and the glorious abundance. The fruit and vegetable stalls provide a riot of colour. Tomatoes, of course, are plentiful: small scarlet ones, some still clinging to their vine; large green-streaked salad tomatoes, craggy and firm; elongated plum tomatoes. They look wonderful to my northerner's eyes, though locals insist that these early summer tomatoes – we were there at the beginning of June – are poor fare. The season proper begins only in late July.

Tunisian aubergines, fat and round, mauve streaked with white, vie for space with the longer, glossy, black-purple 'nostrano' aubergines. The last of the spring globe artichokes sit side by side with their tiny, viciously spiked, wild cousins and the striking Palermitano yellow thorned variety. Courgettes of the type we recognize are overshadowed by the yard-long pale green *zucca longa*, and heaps of *tenerumi*, curling pale green squash tendrils and young leaves, used in soups and risotto.

The scent of cherries, tiny wood strawberries, peaches and nectarines masks the stink of the drains. There are green almonds, milky inside their downy soft shells, and punnets of white and black mulberries which we could not resist, though their flavour is poor compared with ones eaten straight from the tree. On one stall I counted sixteen different types of olive, ranging from the rabbit-dropping-sized, wrinkled, black kind to taut-skinned, juicy, green ones as big as bantam's eggs.

The fishmongers' displays are dominated by massive sides of tuna, the largest from a fish that had weighed in at a good 880 lb (400 kg). Despite the heat and the

Tomato-seller in Il Ballaro Market, Palermo.

apparent lack of refrigeration, the freshness and wide variety of fish and shellfish are a joy to behold. William was in his element.

The one-way system and the nose-to-tail hooting traffic conspire to make driving in Palermo a nightmare, and as soon as we'd had our fill of marketing and sight-seeing we escaped into the peace of the countryside. Long dusty roads, snaking through the wide-open hills and valleys, led us to the country estate of the Marquesa de Tasca-Lanza, at Regaleali. We arrived in the late afternoon, to be greeted not by the grandeur I had expected, but by the sight of Toto the shepherd, milking his flock of lean brown sheep.

Toto learnt his trade from his father, who learnt from his father in turn, and back and back through countless generations. Little seems to have changed in the dairy where the Caciocavallo and ricotta cheeses are made twice a day. We watched as Toto stoked up the fires beneath the well-used copper cauldrons, scalding the rich sheep's milk for the first cheeses and boiling up the whey again (ricotta means 're-cooked') to skim off the soft white curds that are lightly pressed into mounds of fresh ricotta.

A little further up the road the solidly constructed, main cluster of houses looks down over the sweep of the estate, across citrus orchards, fruit trees and vegetable garden down to fields of gilded wheat, vineyards and olive orchards. The old buildings surround a cobbled courtyard, palm tree in one corner for shade from the

The Mattanza

Favignana is a curious little island lying a mile or so off the Sicilian coast near Trapani. It is here that we met a band of piratical, but immensely charming tuna fishermen, who went to great lengths to point out that they weren't actually Sicilian at all, but Favignanans. In appearance they were indeed distinctive, and distinctly un-Sicilian.

Tuna have spawned off the Sicilian coast since time immemorial, providing a regular source of fish that has been tapped since Roman times. They learnt to use this to their advantage. Sprinkled along the coast are a number of fish traps (now dramatically fewer than even ten years ago) set in the path of the migrating fish; when these are drawn in, the tuna are landed. This, broadly, is the *mattanza* (the English word 'slaughter' is not an easy equivalent, being too judgemental).

Perhaps inevitably for Sicily, there is far more to all this than a simple fish trap in the sea. The whole fishery is carefully controlled by the undisputed and highly respected *reis*, or king, a name echoing the distant Arabic origins of much of the Sicilian dialect. He it is who authorizes the *mattanza*, and he it is who stands at the head of the hierarchy that supports and controls both the local fishery and the community. Each time the traps are visited by either divers or fishermen, there is an elaborate procession of boats towards the nets, and everyone who goes will, without exception, get a few pounds of fresh tuna meat from the trap.

The *mattanza* itself is a bloody affair. The fish are gaffed into flat-bottomed barges whose design allows a long line of fishermen to work together without tipping the boat over. Gradually the net is drawn in until the fish inside are inexorably drawn to the surface. The sight of a whole seething mass of tuna is quite unforgettable, though their killing, to many, is shockingly barbaric.

Here in Favignana a community is being forced to adapt to circumstances beyond its control, for the bluefin tuna is a threatened species. Although it is pursued along all of its migratory course, stocks of this fish were, until quite recently, adequate. But ferocious demand from Japan has changed everything. The harsh reality is that such communities cannot expect to live off fish any more whether fishing of the bluefin is totally banned or not. But let's hope that they can adapt and not just die.

mid-day sunshine, magenta roses scaling the walls. It was here that we ate lunch for the next few days, relishing the vast array of vegetable anti-pasti that the Marquesa and her cook Maria conjured up for us.

A few years ago I was sent a copy of a book called *Sicilian Food* (published by Century Books, but already out of print), which is undoubtedly the most fascinating, scholarly, entertaining and practical book on the cooking of the island; in fact, a classic among cookery books. To my delight its American author, Mary Simetti Taylor, a long-time resident of Sicily, had agreed to spare us a few days of her time.

Sicily is full of almond trees, a glorious sight in February when they come into blossom. The nuts themselves, harvested in the autumn, are full and plump and sweet. They form the basis of Sicily's most specialized confectionary, *pasta reale* (marzipan). Mary took us to the medieval town of Erice, perched high up on a cliff above the plain, where she knows two practitioners of the art of making *pasta reale*.

Both Maria Grammatico, who runs her own shop, and Ninetta, whose surname I never discovered, learnt their skill from the nuns of the Convent of San Carlo, now defunct, the buildings housing an art gallery instead of holy confectioners. In her shop Maria has an enticing display of *frutta di Martorana*, life-like marzipan fruit, which take their name from the Palermitano monastery of Martorana, another convent that has disappeared.

Ninetta is famed for her larger-scale marzipan 'cakes', pascal lambs for Easter, flaming hearts and other designs, moulded and painted by hand in the window of her small dining room.

On Sunday we stayed closer to Alcamo, Mary's adopted home, visited her neighbours, Irene and Vito Ruvola, from whom she'd learnt much about feasting and food. Every Sunday the grown-up children and the grandchildren appear for a riotous lunch. We were to be more than twenty at table, and that was a lot of work for the cooks.

Irene and her sister-in-law Pina had started the day before, making the macaroni, or rather *busiata* – egg pasta rolled by hand round dried reeds (*busi*). Not that they'd finished by any means, and as soon as we arrived Mary and I were roped in to help. By the time we'd completed the job I was turning out moderately presentable *busiate* for a beginner.

The long trestle-tables were laid out on the terrace. Baskets were filled full of fruit from the orchard at the back of the house – black juicy mulberries, cherries and peaches. Lunch began late, and by the time we'd finished, having worked our way through pasta, meat, salad and several rounds of puddings, it was already early evening. We crept away, sated and sleepy.

ⓥ
Carciofini a Spezzatino
Braised Artichokes in Olive Oil

Spezzatino *just means 'cut up into chunks', and it's one of several names given to this dish of lightly stewed artichokes. Other names that I came across were 'alla contadina' (farmer's style), and 'alla villanella' (peasant style). Whatever you care to call it, it is probably the most widespread way of cooking artichokes on the island.*

The Marquesa, who made it for us, serves the tender curves of artichoke cold as part of an anti-pasto, though I have to admit to liking them warm, or even hot on pasta.

SERVES 4

4 large or 6–8 small artichokes	2 cloves garlic, chopped
1 lemon	4 tablespoons chopped fresh parsley
4 tablespoons olive oil	salt
1 red onion, chopped	pinch of chilli flakes or black pepper

Preparing the artichokes is the most onerous part of this recipe. Begin by acidulating a pint (600 ml) or so of water with the juice of the lemon, and drop the squeezed lemon halves in as well. Now for the work. Snap off the stalk at the base of each artichoke. Then, working round, snap off the leaves close to the base, continuing until you reach the more tender ones at the heart. With a sharp knife trim off the bottoms of the leaves you've snapped off, leaving just the base of the artichoke.

Slice off the cone of tender leaves about ½ inch (1 cm) above the base. Dip the artichoke in the acidulated water occasionally as you work to prevent browning. With the tip of your knife, or a teaspoon, scrape the hairy choke from the centre of the artichoke and discard it. Finally cut the prepared base into 8 wedges if it is a large one, or 4 if it is small, and drop these into the acidulated water.

On to the easy part. Place the olive oil, onion and garlic into a pan large enough to take all the artichokes as well. Set over a medium heat and cook until the onion is translucent, without letting it brown. Add the artichokes and stir and fry for a minute or so more. Now add enough water or light stock to come about half-way up the artichoke pieces, the parsley, salt and chilli flakes. Bring to the boil, reduce the heat, cover and cook for about 10–15 minutes, until tender. Serve hot or cold.

ⓥ
Pomodori Ripieni
Stuffed Tomatoes

The Marquesa's stuffed tomatoes pick up on another classic Sicilian mixture of flavours, currants and pine nuts, here with the sharpness of capers and the saltiness of black olives. So widespread is the currant-and-pine-nut combo that they are sold ready-mixed in small sachets in markets and food shops, though it has to be said that it's a mean ratio of a minimal number of expensive pine nuts to an overload of cheaper currants. Better, in the end, to mix them yourself.

SERVES 4

4 medium tomatoes
salt
½ tablespoon olive oil

Stuffing

1 small red onion, finely chopped
2 cloves garlic, finely chopped
2–3 tablespoons olive oil
1½ oz (40 g) stale fine breadcrumbs
1 oz (25 g) pitted black olives, finely
    chopped

1 tablespoon capers, roughly chopped
1½ tablespoons currants
1 tablespoon pine nuts
2 tablespoons chopped fresh parsley
salt and pepper

Cut the tops off the tomatoes and scoop out the flesh (save the tops and flesh for making sauce). Season the insides with a little salt and leave upside down on a wire rack to drain for 30 minutes or so, while you make the stuffing.

Pre-heat the oven to 400°F (200°C), gas mark 6.

Place the onion, garlic and olive oil in a frying-pan and cook over a medium heat until the onion is tender. Add the breadcrumbs, raise the heat slightly and fry until golden-brown (add a little extra oil if necessary). Scoop out into a bowl and mix with all the remaining stuffing ingredients.

Pack the stuffing into the tomatoes and snuggle them together in an oiled ovenproof dish. Drizzle ½ tablespoon oil over the tomatoes. Bake in the oven for about 15 minutes, until nicely browned.

Ⓥ

Melanzane alla Parmigiana
Baked Aubergine with Tomato Sauce

Though this is made all over Italy, the Sicilians claim it as their own. I brazenly suggested to the Marquesa, as she was layering the aubergine with the tomato sauce, that the name implied a more northerly origin in the town of Parma. Nonsense! The name is merely incidental, a corruption of some older Sicilian dialect word. Wherever it comes from, Melanzane alla Parmigiana *is a superb dish, good as a starter or as a main course.*

If you want to cut down a little on the oiliness, grill the aubergine slices (brushed lightly with olive oil first) instead of frying them: not authentic, but an alternative worth trying once or twice.

SERVES 4 as a main course –
or 6–8 as a first course

2 large aubergines
salt and pepper
plenty of olive oil and/or sunflower oil
  for frying

1 pint (600 ml) tomato sauce (see p.89)
10 fresh basil leaves, roughly torn up
1 teaspoon dried oregano
2 oz (50 g) Parmesan cheese, grated

Cut the aubergines lengthways into slices about ½–¾ inch (1–2 cm) thick. Spread out on trays or dishes, sprinkle with salt and leave to degorge for at least 30 minutes and up to 2 hours. Rinse and pat dry.

Pre-heat the oven to 400°F (200°C), gas mark 6.

Heat a 1-inch (2.5-cm)-deep layer of olive oil, or olive oil mixed with sunflower oil, in a wide frying-pan over a moderate heat. Fry the aubergine slices in batches in the oil until golden-brown. Once done, lift out and drain on kitchen paper.

Find a baking dish large enough to take the aubergine slices in 3 or 4 layers. Spread a thin layer of tomato sauce on the base. Cover with aubergine slices. Spread over more of the tomato sauce, season with salt and pepper, dot with a scant third of the basil leaves, sprinkle over a little oregano and about a quarter of the Parmesan cheese. Repeat these layers twice more, using up the tomato sauce, basil and Parmesan completely on the last layer. Bake in the oven for 20 minutes, until browned and bubbling. Serve hot, warm or cold.

Salsa di Pomodoro
Tomato Sauce

I offer you three alternatives here, all of them turning out a very good, relatively smooth tomato sauce, with allowances for the lesser quality of North European tomatoes. Tomato Purée and a little sugar compensate to some degree, and so too does generous seasoning.

The first is the kind of sauce to make in high summer, when fresh tomatoes are at their cheapest, ripest and sweetest. At other times of the year passata *(sieved tomato purée) is a perfectly acceptable alternative. In Sicily most households make enough* passata *to last them through the winter, crammed into wine bottles and sterilized so it will keep. The* passata *or 'creamed tomatoes' that is sold here in bottles or cartons in most supermarkets is pretty good.*

The other tomato preserve made all over the island is estratto, *an immensely thick and salty, semi-dried tomato paste. The concentrated caramelized flavour adds a marvellous depth to sauces. The nearest I can get to it is a mixture of sun-dried tomato and tomato purée.*

MAKES about 1 pint (600 ml)

With Fresh Tomatoes

2 lb (900 g) ripe tomatoes, skinned and
    seeded
1 large onion, chopped
3 cloves garlic, chopped
3 tablespoons olive oil

2 tablespoons tomato purée
½–1 tablespoon sugar
salt and pepper
3 sprigs of fresh basil

Liquidize or process the tomatoes. Place the onion, garlic and olive oil in a large pan and cook over a medium heat until the onion is tender. Add the processed tomatoes, tomato purée, sugar, salt and pepper and simmer gently for 30 minutes. Now add the basil and cook for a further 5–10 minutes. Taste and add a little more sugar if the sauce is on the sharp side. Adjust the seasoning. Before using, remove the sprigs of basil.

With *Passata*

Make as above, substituting 1 pint (600 ml) *passata* for the processed tomatoes

With *Estratto* (or as Near as You Can Get)

Make as above. Use the same quantity of fresh tomatoes or *passata*, but make the tomato purée as follows: process 4 tablespoons tomato purée with 2 oz (50 g) roughly chopped sun-dried tomatoes preserved in olive oil and add to the sauce along with the tomatoes.

Ⓥ

Melanzane sott'Olio
Aubergines Preserved in Olive Oil

I kept picking at the Marquesa's aubergine preserves, which she had left out on the table. As she wanted to serve them at lunchtime I forced myself to stop before they were all gone.

When aubergines are cheap in the summer, this is a lovely way to stash them away for later in the year. Serve them alongside cheeses and salamis as part of an anti-pasto. Be warned: the four large aubergines end up reduced to a mere fraction of their original presence.

MAKES 2–3 ½ lb (225 g) jars

4 large aubergines
3 fl oz (85 ml) white wine vinegar
2 tablespoons salt

2–4 dried red chillies, snapped in half
1 heaped tablespoon dried oregano
olive oil to cover

Peel the aubergines and shred coarsely. Mix with the vinegar and salt and place a plate on top to weight them down. Leave overnight, or for at least 8 hours, then drain well. Squeeze bone dry in clean tea-towels, then pack into cool sterilized jars (see p.79), tucking in the dried chillies and sprinkling with oregano as you go. Pour in enough oil to cover completely. Cover with a cloth and let the jars stand for 1 hour to settle. If necessary, top up with more oil, then seal tightly. Leave in a cool dark place for at least 3 weeks before eating.

Ⓥ

Caponata
Sweet-and-sour Aubergine

I can think of no other cold aubergine dish that surpasses Caponata *I've been making it for years, but was rather upset to learn that I'd been getting it wrong! In Sicily they use green olives in* Caponata, *not black as I always do. So, if you want to do it properly, use green ones — though, to be honest, I'm going to continue in my same mistaken way. Serve* Caponata *as part of an anti-pasto, or as a cross between a relish and a side-dish.*

SERVES 4–6

1 large aubergine, diced
6 tablespoons olive oil
6 sticks celery, chopped
1 onion, chopped
1 × 14 oz (400 g) tin chopped tomatoes or
    1 lb (450 g) fresh tomatoes, skinned
    and chopped
2 tablespoons caster sugar

4 tablespoons red wine vinegar
1 teaspoon grated nutmeg
1 heaped teaspoon capers
12 green or black olives, pitted and
    roughly chopped
2 tablespoons chopped fresh parsley
salt and pepper

Spread out the aubergine dice in a colander, sprinkle with salt and set aside for ½ – 1 hour. Press gently to extract as much water as possible. Dry on kitchen paper or a clean tea-towel.

Heat 4 tablespoons of the olive oil in a heavy-based frying-pan. Sauté the celery until browned. Scoop out and set aside. Fry the aubergine in the same oil until browned and tender, adding a little extra oil if necessary. Scoop out and leave to cool.

Add the remaining oil to the pan and sauté the onion until golden. Add the tomatoes and simmer for 15 minutes until thick. Next add the sugar, vinegar and nutmeg and cook for a further 10 minutes, until you have a rich sweet-and-sour sauce. Add a little salt and plenty of pepper. Stir in the capers, olives, parsley, aubergine and celery. Taste and adjust the seasoning – the flavours will soften as the *caponata* cools. Serve in a dish when cool.

Ⓥ

Cipolline in Agrodolce
Sweet-and-sour Pearl Onions

There are many agrodolce *(sweet-and-sour dishes) in Sicilian cookery, often picking up on the natural sweetness of vegetables. Though these little sweet-and-sour onions are usually part and parcel of the anti-pasto selection, they also go very well with cold meats, such as ham, or even with a nice piece of mature Cheddar! – not remotely a Sicilian combination, but worth trying anyway. Once cooked, they will keep, covered of course, in the refrigerator for three or four days.*

SERVES 4–6

1½ lb (750 g) pearl onions	1 bay leaf
2 tablespoons olive oil	2 sprigs of fresh thyme
4 tablespoons tomato purée	salt and pepper
2 tablespoons caster or granulated sugar	1½ tablespoons chopped fresh parsley
3 tablespoons red or white wine vinegar	

To skin the onions, first top and tail them, then cover with boiling water. Leave for 1 – 2 minutes, drain and slip off the skins. Dry on kitchen paper.

Heat the oil in a wide frying-pan and add the onions. Brown briskly, then add all the remaining ingredients except the parsley. Pour in enough water to cover the onions. Bring to the boil, reduce the heat and half-cover. Simmer gently for 40 – 45 minutes, stirring occasionally, until the onions are tender and bathed in a sweet-and-sour sauce. Serve cold, sprinkled with parsley.

ⓥ
Insalata Cotta
Cooked Salad

Nobody much wants to have the oven on for long periods of time in the fearsome heat of high summer, assuming that they have an oven at all. The prospect is even more unwelcome in the crowded residential areas of Palermo. There's plenty of call for purveyors of street-food. In the markets, shoppers can buy ready-baked onions and boiled potatoes to make an Insalata Cotta, *literally a 'cooked salad'. To the standard onion/potato duo is added whatever is to hand. This is what one market vendor told me he liked in his* Insalata Cotta.

SERVES 4

3 large round flat onions
12 oz (350 g) slightly waxy potatoes, boiled and peeled
8 oz (225 g) green beans, lightly cooked and cut in half

1 lb (450 g) tomatoes, roughly cut up
5 tablespoons olive oil
1½ tablespoons white wine vinegar
1½ teaspoons dried oregano
salt and pepper

Pre-heat the oven to 375°F (190°C), gas mark 5. Trim the onions, but do not peel. Boil the onions in water for 10 minutes and drain well. Then bake in the oven in an oiled ovenproof dish, uncovered, for about 1 hour, until well-browned and very tender. Cool.

To make the salad, pull the skins off the onions and cut up the flesh roughly. Cut the potatoes into chunks and mix with the onions and remaining ingredients. Taste and adjust the seasoning.

Ⓥ
Arancini
Fried Stuffed Rice Balls

Arancini which literally means little oranges, have long been one of my favourite snacks when I'm in the south of Italy. You can always get them at railway station buffets, and often at cafés. They are a little fiddly to make at home, but worth it in my book. Though they taste best when hot, they're not at all bad cold – just the thing for a picnic or packed lunch.

MAKES 12

12 oz (350 g) risotto rice (such as arborio)
salt, pepper and nutmeg
4 eggs
3 oz (75 g) Caciocavallo or Parmesan
    cheese, freshly grated
1 oz (25 g) butter
5 tablespoons very thick tomato sauce
    (see p.89)

2 oz (50 g) green peas (shelled weight),
    cooked
2 oz (50 g) Mozzarella cheese, cubed
flour
3 oz (75 g) fine dry breadcrumbs
sunflower or vegetable oil for deep-frying

Cook the rice in plenty of boiling salted water until tender. Drain thoroughly. Mix with 2 of the eggs, the Caciocavallo or Parmesan cheese, the butter, salt, pepper and nutmeg. Work well with your hands until the mixture holds together, then leave to cool. Meanwhile simmer the tomato sauce and peas together for 5 minutes, then leave to cool.

Working on one at a time, divide the rice into 12 portions and roll into balls (wet your hands first to prevent sticking). Make a fairly capacious hole in the centre with your finger and insert a teaspoonful of the tomato/pea mixture and a cube of Mozzarella. Carefully cover the filling with a knob of rice, sealing it in completely. Mould back into a ball.

Beat the remaining eggs lightly. Roll the *Arancini* first in flour, then dip into beaten egg, shaking off the excess, and finally roll in breadcrumbs, making sure that each one is thoroughly and evenly coated. Deep-fry a few balls at a time in plenty of oil, pre-heated to about 325°F (160°C), until richly browned. Drain on kitchen paper. Serve hot or warm.

To re-heat, either pop back into the oil for a few minutes or heat through, uncovered, in a warm oven.

Ⓥ
Pasta con le Melanzane
Pasta with Fried Aubergine

Once the individual elements of this dish are prepared, the rest is largely diy in the Ruvolo household. Pasta and tomato sauce are dished out at the head of the table, then each member of the family helps himself or herself to aubergine, cheese and herbs from the bowls that are laid out down the long table.

SERVES 6

2 large aubergines
salt
plenty of olive oil for frying
1½ lb (750 g) macaroni or thick spaghetti
tomato sauce from cooking *Bracioline*
    (p.102) or made to the recipe on p.89

freshly grated pecorino or Parmesan
    cheese
fresh basil leaves
roughly chopped fresh parsley

Cut the aubergines into discs about ½ inch (1 cm) thick. Lay out on a baking sheet or large dish and sprinkle with salt. Leave for 30 minutes – 1 hour to degorge. Rinse and pat dry. Fry briskly in plenty of olive oil until nicely browned, then drain on kitchen paper.

Throw the pasta in a huge pot of vigorously boiling, salted water, bring back to the boil and cook until *al dente*. Drain and tip into a large bowl, add a slug of olive oil and turn to coat. Meanwhile re-heat the tomato sauce. Spoon a little over the pasta. Transfer the aubergine (it's fine if it's tepid or even cold) to a serving dish and put the cheese, basil leaves and parsley into separate small bowls.

At the table serve everyone with pasta and tomato sauce, and let them help themselves to the rest.

Ⓥ
Pesto Ericinese
Basil, Almond and Tomato Pesto

The Sicilians have their own version of the more famous Genoese sauce, pesto. Like its namesake it is perfumed with basil and garlic and incorporates plenty of pungent cheese, but takes almonds rather than pine nuts as a basis and smooths the whole lot out with plenty of tomatoes.

The traditional method of making it demands strong arm muscles, but many think that the flavour and texture produced by this method are superior. I usually opt for the processor method, which takes only a few minutes, and I don't honestly believe that the difference is that remarkable.

Toss the Pesto Ericinese *into piping-hot pasta – spaghetti* or tagliatelle *or whatever takes your fancy – and serve with extra grated cheese for those who want it.*

SERVES 4 on pasta

1½ oz (40 g) fresh basil leaves
3 cloves garlic
½ teaspoon salt
4 oz (100 g) blanched almonds, roughly chopped
2 oz (50 g) Caciocavallo, pecorino or Parmesan cheese, freshly grated

12 oz (350 g) tomatoes, skinned, seeded and roughly chopped
1 tablespoon tomato purée (optional)
1 level teaspoon sugar (optional)
3 fl oz (85 ml) olive oil
pepper

There are two ways of making this: the traditional and the processor method.

Traditional method

Pound the basil, garlic and salt to a paste in a mortar. Gradually add the almonds, working them into the paste, followed by the cheese. Next add the chopped tomato and work that all to a pulp. Finally stir in the tomato purée and sugar if using (British tomatoes may well need their help), the olive oil and pepper. Taste and add more salt if necessary.

Processor method

Place the basil leaves, garlic (roughly chopped), salt, almonds and cheese in the processor and process to a rough paste. Add the tomatoes, tomato purée and sugar (if using) and pepper and process again, gradually trickling in the olive oil. Taste and add salt if needed.

Tagliatelle con Fave e Pancetta
Tagliatelle with Broad Beans and Pancetta

Maria, the cook at Regaleali, prepared this marvellous pasta dish for us on our last day there. It was one of the best things we ate in Sicily, though it is surprisingly simple. The pasta was followed with fried calf's liver, a salad and a bowl of freshly picked cherries: a perfect meal.

If you use fresh tagliatelle, *which take only a few minutes to cook, start warming the oil before you put the pasta in the boiling water.*

SERVES 4 generously

1 lb (450 g) broad beans (shelled weight), thawed if frozen
1 lb (450 g) *tagliatelle*
salt and pepper
5 tablespoons olive oil
2 cloves garlic, sliced

6 oz (175 g) *pancetta* or streaky bacon, rinded and cut into thin strips
1½ oz (40 g) Parmesan cheese, freshly grated
2 tablespoons chopped fresh parsley

First prepare the broad beans. If they have been frozen, just let them thaw, then, using a small sharp knife, slit the outer skins and squeeze out the bright green inner beans. With fresh broad beans, blanch for 1 minute in boiling water, drain and cool quickly in cold running water. Remove the skins as for frozen beans, then cook in fresh water until barely done. Drain well.

Bring a big pot of salted water to the boil and add the *tagliatelle*. Boil until *al dente* in the usual way.

As soon as the pasta is in the pot, put the olive oil and garlic into a wide frying-pan over a moderate heat. Cook until the garlic is beginning to brown, then scoop it out. Immediately add the *pancetta* and broad beans. Fry gently over a low heat, stirring from time to time, until the *tagliatelle* are ready (it's fine if the beans go slightly fuzzy at the edges, just as long as they don't burn!). Drain the *tagliatelle* and tip into a warmed serving bowl. Immediately pour over the contents of the frying-pan. Add the Parmesan, parsley, salt and pepper to taste, and toss. Serve straight away.

Sarde a Beccaficu
Sardines Stuffed with Currants and Pine Nuts

To the uninitiated this reads as Sicily's most baroque and unfathomable of dishes – sardines with dried currants and pine nuts and orange juice? Put aside any prejudices and try it, because it is a genuine triumph. Once the sardines are boned – not difficult when you get the knack – the rest is easy going, and the stuffed sardines take no time at all to cook. I happen to like them hot, but it is more correct, I am told, to leave them to cool.

SERVES 4

12 small sardines, scaled and cleaned
3 oz (75 g) stale white breadcrumbs
4 tablespoons olive oil
2 oz (50 g) currants, soaked in warm water
    for 10 minutes and drained
2 oz (50 g) pine nuts
6 tinned anchovy fillets, finely chopped

2 tablespoons finely chopped fresh parsley
salt and pepper
6 bay leaves
juice of ½ lemon
juice of ½ orange
orange wedges to serve

Pre-heat the oven to 350°F (180°C), gas mark 4.

The first task is to bone the sardines. Cut off the heads and dorsal fins and discard. Extend the cut along the belly right down to the tail end of each fish with a small knife. Open out the flaps and sit the fish on its belly with its back upwards. Press firmly down along the backbone with the heel of your hand, flattening the fish out. Turn it over and pull out the backbone. Rinse the fish and pat dry.

Brown the breadcrumbs in 2½ tablespoons of the olive oil over a low heat, stirring constantly. Draw off the heat and add the drained currants, pine nuts, chopped anchovies, parsley and some pepper. Lay the sardines cut side up, put a generous teaspoon of the filling on the wide end of each one and roll up towards the tail. Place in an oiled heatproof dish with the tails sticking up in the air, packing them in fairly tightly so that they don't unwind. Tuck the bay leaves in among them. Sprinkle over the lemon and orange juice and the remaining oil and season with salt and pepper. Bake in the oven for 15–25 minutes, until just cooked through. Serve hot or cold with extra orange wedges.

OVERLEAF
Left: *Tagliatelle con fave e pancetta* (Tagliatelle with Broad Beans
and Pancetta) see p.96. Right: *Sarde a beccaficu* (Sardines Stuffed with
Currants and Pine Nuts) see p.97.

Tonno al Salmoriglio
Grilled Marinated Tuna

William's friend, the tuna fisherman Joaquino, showed him how they liked to eat tuna on the island of Favignana. They'd completed a successful mattanza *(see p.84) the day before, and there was plenty of incredibly fresh tuna to be had. Salmoriglio is the name given to the simple, fresh-tasting marinade of lemon juice, olive oil, garlic and oregano. When it comes to the grilling part, treat the tuna a little like steak, leaving it pink and juicy in the centre.*

SERVES 4

2 lb (900 g) tuna steaks, about ¾ inch (2 cm) thick	salt and pepper
juice of 1 large lemon	1 tablespoon dried oregano
8 tablespoons olive oil	1 clove garlic, crushed (optional)
	lemon wedges to serve

Divide the tuna into 4 portions if necessary, discarding the skin. Whisk the lemon juice with the olive oil, salt and pepper, then stir in the oregano and garlic if using. Pour over the tuna steaks and leave to marinate for at least 30 minutes, but preferably for a good 1−2 hours turning once or twice.

Take the steaks out of the marinade and grill them, close to the heat, for about 4 minutes on each side, until browned outside but still slightly pink at the centre. Serve immediately with lemon wedges.

Tonno con Acciughe e Pomodoro
Seared Tuna with Anchovy and Tomato Sauce

I must be truthful about this recipe. It doesn't come from Sicily at all, but has more to do with my kitchen at home in north London. Still, I feel justified in including it, because it has a truly southern Mediterranean twang and certainly uses ingredients that abound in Sicily.

In this recipe the tuna is cooked rare, like steak, so that it retains its moistness and fresh flavour. The simple anchovy and tomato sauce makes a great partner.

SERVES 4

2 lb (900 g) tuna steaks, about ¾ inch (2 cm) thick	6 tinned anchovy fillets, roughly chopped
juice of ½ lemon	2 cloves garlic, finely chopped
5 fl oz (150 ml) olive oil	2 tomatoes, seeded and diced small
salt and pepper	2 tablespoons chopped fresh parsley

Divide the tuna into 4 portions and marinate in the lemon juice, 4 tablespoons of the olive oil, salt and pepper, for at least 30 minutes.

Begin the sauce while you wait. Warm the remaining oil in a small saucepan and add the anchovies and garlic. Cook over a low heat, mashing in the anchovies with a fork, until they have melted down and the garlic is lightly browned. Draw off the heat.

To cook the tuna, grease a heavy-based frying-pan with a little hot oil, then set over a high heat for about 5 minutes until searingly hot. Shake the excess marinade from the tuna and slap the pieces on to the hot metal (you may have to do this in 2 batches). Leave for 1 minute, then turn over and give the other side a minute too. With a sharp knife check the interior, which should still be rosy pink at the heart. If it is just too raw for your liking, reduce the heat and cook for a little longer.

As soon as the tuna is done, transfer it to a warm serving dish and keep warm. Add the tomato dice and parsley to the anchovy sauce, re-heat briefly and spoon over the tuna. Serve immediately.

Tonno in Agrodolce
Tuna with Sweet-and-sour Onions

We ate tuna slathered with sweet-and-sour onions in a small restaurant just off one of Palermo's main streets. It was a stickily hot night, and the traffic fumes and noise swirled around us – not that we noticed a great deal, as the meal was so good, particularly this dish. The sharp sweet onions set off the richness of tuna perfectly.

SERVES 4

1½–2 lb (750–900 g) tuna steaks, about ¾ inch (2 cm) thick	1 level tablespoon caster sugar
salt and pepper	3 tablespoons red wine vinegar
4 tablespoons olive oil	3 fl oz (85 ml) dry white wine
2 large onions, thinly sliced	2 tablespoons chopped fresh parsley

Divide the tuna into 4 portions (if necessary) and season with salt and pepper.

Warm 3 tablespoons of the olive oil in a wide frying-pan and add the onions. Cook gently until soft, then raise the heat to medium and fry until richly browned. Scoop out and reserve.

Add the remaining oil to the pan and heat thoroughly. Fry the tuna steaks briskly on both sides to brown. Reduce the heat and cook for a further 1 minute. Now add the sugar, vinegar and wine and return the onions to the pan. Stir around the tuna, turn the heat up high, cover and simmer for a final 2 minutes. Sprinkle with parsley and serve.

Bracioline
Sicilian Beef Olives

Irene, Pina and I had a high old time rolling up the Bracioline, *thin slices of beef wrapped around a filling of cheese, eggs and* mortadella. *We had to remember that one member of the family didn't like* Caciocavallo *cheese, so had to have Gruyère instead and that another didn't like cheese at all, so one of these hefty beef olives must be made rather slimmer than the rest, and then we had to mark the relevant exceptions to the rule with flags of extra herbs, so that we would be able to tell them from the rest when it came to dishing up.*

The Bracioline *are in fact a small version of the more common Sicilian* Braciolone, *one single giant beef roll with an even more complex mixture of ingredients wrapped up inside. They are cooked in plenty of tomato sauce, ensuring that there is not only enough to moisten the cooked rolls themselves, but also sufficient to serve with pasta as a first course – two dishes in one.*

SERVES 6–8

6 large thin slices beef (such as topside), measuring a good 10 × 6 inches (25 × 15 cm)	1 bunch of fresh parsley
salt and pepper	3–5 oz (75–150 g) *Caciocavallo* or Gruyère cheese, cut into thick batons
12 thin slices *mortadella*	1 onion, cut into 6 wedges
3 oz (75 g) pork fat, cut into strips	6 hard-boiled eggs, shelled

Sauce

4 tablespoons olive oil	2 bay leaves
1 large onion, chopped	½ head of garlic, divided into individual cloves and peeled
1½ pints (900 ml) *passata*	6 sprigs of fresh basil
3 tablespoons tomato purée	salt and pepper
2 teaspoons sugar	

Lay the slices of beef out in pairs on the work surface, overlapping each pair by about 1 inch (2.5 cms) along the wide edge, to give 3 'rectangles' roughly 10 × 11 inches (25 × 28 cm). Season with salt and pepper.

Now start building up the filling. Cover each rectangle with 4 pieces of *mortadella*. Lay the remaining ingredients in a band along one of the long sides, leaving a border of about 1½ inches (4 cm). Begin with a line of pork fat, then snuggle 3 or 4 sprigs of parsley up against the fat. Next add a third of the cheese, a couple of wedges of onion and finally 2 of the hard-boiled eggs.

Now comes the tricky part. Starting from one of the long sides, roll up the beef around the filling, flipping the borders in to cover it as you go, and keeping it all tight and compact. Quickly tie each roll up firmly with string, winding it round to hold everything together.

In a pan large enough to take all 3 rolls in a single layer, warm the olive oil from the sauce ingredients over a brisk heat. Brown the rolls all over in the oil, then take them out of the pan and reduce the heat. Cook the chopped onion gently in the same oil until translucent. Return the rolls to the pan along with all the remaining sauce ingredients and add enough water to cover the meat. Bring to the boil, reduce the heat, half-cover and simmer very gently for 2–2½ hours. Stir occasionally, and make sure that the sauce is not catching or over-reducing. If necessary, add a little water to thin it down.

Once cooked, the richly flavoured tomato sauce is used to dress pasta (see the recipe on p.94), while the beef rolls are kept warm, moistened with just a spoonful or two of the sauce, and covered to prevent drying out.

Just before serving, snip off the string and slice thickly.

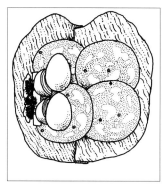

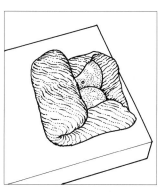

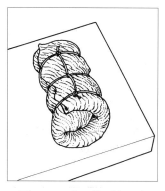

1 Lay out two of the slices of beef overlapping the long edges by 1 inch (2.5 cm). Cover with *mortadella* and lay the pork fat, parsley, *caciocavallo*, onion and 2 eggs along the long edge leaving margins on the side and back edges.

2 Roll up the filling inside the beef flipping over the side edges as you go.

3 Tie up each roll with string winding it round to hold everything together.

The Taxi-Driver's Coniglio a Cacciatora
Hunter's Rabbit

Ask any Sicilian about what dishes they like to eat, and you'll get a lengthy and detailed reply. My taxi-driver was no exception. His favourite dish was Sarde a Beccaficu *(Sardines stuffed with currants and pine nuts), closely followed by* Coniglio a Cacciatora. *Just in time I dug a pen from the bottom of my bag and managed to make a note of his recipe. Whether he would approve of my interpretation, I don't know, but we thought it was really good.*

SERVES 4

1 rabbit, cut into 8 joints
2 tablespoons white wine vinegar
seasoned flour
3 tablespoons olive oil
3 sticks celery, diced
3 cloves garlic, sliced
2 tablespoons tomato purée

10 fl oz (300 ml) *passata* or sieved fresh tomatoes
1 generous glass red wine
salt and pepper
2 oz (50 g) pitted green olives
3 oz (75 g) raisins
1½ oz (40 g) pine nuts
1½ tablespoons chopped fresh parsley

Rub the rabbit all over with the wine vinegar, cover and leave overnight (this is really for wild rabbit, but it improves domesticated as well). Drain and dust with seasoned flour.

Heat the olive oil in a heatproof casserole and brown the rabbit pieces briskly. Add the celery, garlic, tomato purée, *passata*, red wine, salt and pepper, then 5 fl oz (150 ml) water. Bring to a simmer, half-cover and stew very gently for 1 – 1½ hours, turning occasionally, until the meat is tender. Add the remaining ingredients and cook, uncovered, for a further 10 minutes before serving.

ⓥ Sorbetto di Fragola
Strawberry Sorbet

Many of the scruffiest of cafés in Palermo's back streets make their own ice-creams and sorbets, blending and freezing them virtually on the pavement as you watch. They are more than welcome on a hot day, as long as the lack of hygiene doesn't bother you too much.

We gave in to the lure of cooling scoops of strawberry sorbet, intensely flavoured as only a freshly made water-ice, based on sun-ripened fruit, can be. The formula is straightforward — it's the quality of the fruit that counts. You need the best strawberries, their sweet scent balanced with a hint of tartness. If you can find them, throw in a handful of tiny wood strawberries as well, or serve alongside the finished sorbet.

SERVES 4–6

5 oz (150 g) sugar
1 lb (450 g) strawberries, hulled and
    halved
juice of 1 orange

Put the sugar in a pan with 4 fl oz (120 ml) water and stir over a medium heat until the sugar has dissolved. Bring to the boil, then draw off the heat and cool.

Process the strawberries with the orange juice and about two-thirds of the sugar syrup. Taste and add more syrup if necessary, bearing in mind that the sweetness will be dulled when the sorbet is frozen. The mixture should be a little on the sweet side, but not overwhelmingly sugary.

Freeze in a sorbetière if you have one. If not, set the freezer to its coldest setting. Pour the mixture into a shallow freezer container and freeze until the sides have set. Break up, and push into the centre. Freeze again until beginning to set right through. Quickly tip into a food processor and whizz to a smooth slush, or beat vigorously to smooth out the ice crystals. If you have time, repeat this process once more. Finally return the iced slush to the freezer to finish freezing. Transfer to the refrigerator to soften slightly about 15 minutes before serving.

ⓥ Granita di Fragola
Strawberry Granita

Prepare as above. Freeze the mixture until the sides are beginning to set. Break up into small granules and push into the centre. Repeat this every 30 minutes or so, until you end up with a heap of tiny glittering shards of chilled strawberry ice.

Ⓥ

Biancomangiare
Blancmange

Blancmange it may be, but Biancomangiare *tastes infinitely better than that palid nursery stuff that we get all too often here. Use the best creamiest milk – there's really no point in making it if you try to cut down on the fat by substituting skimmed milk – and the zest of a nicely scented lemon.*

I like the Biancomangiare *just as it is, perhaps with a few raspberries or strawberries on the side, but Irene and Pina often use it instead of ricotta in their* Cassatedde.

SERVES 4–6

1 pint (600 ml) creamy milk
1½ oz (45 g) cornflour
4 oz (100 g) caster sugar
1 strip of lemon zest

Add a few tablespoons of milk to the cornflour in a small bowl and mix to a smooth paste, beating out any lumps. Gradually stir in a little more of the milk until you have a runny cream. Tip into a heavy pan and stir in the remaining milk, sugar and lemon zest. Stir over a low flame, without letting the milk boil, until the mixture is very thick. Draw off the heat and pour into a bowl rinsed out with cold water, or brushed with almond oil (if you wish to turn out the *Biancomangiare*), or into a shallow serving dish. Leave to cool.

Serve with strawberries or raspberries, or use as a filling for pastries.

Cassatedde di Ricotta
Ricotta and Chocolate Fritters

As far as William was concerned, these fritters were the crowning glory of our lengthy Sunday lunch with the Ruvolas, and he couldn't wait for me to make them when we came home. They are sensational, it must be said. Eat them warm, when they no longer burn the mouth, but while the filling of ricotta and chocolate is still runny. They still taste marvellous when they've cooled down, but they don't have quite that irresistibly wicked quality to them.

MAKES around 30 – enough
for 8 – 10 people

sunflower oil for frying
caster sugar

Pasta frolla

1 lb (450 g) plain flour	5 oz (150 g) butter
3 teaspoons baking powder	5 oz (150 g) lard
5 oz (150 g) caster sugar	5 fl oz (150 ml) white wine

Filling

1 lb (450 g) ricotta cheese	1 level teaspoon salt
5 tablespoons milk	8 oz (225 g) plain chocolate,
4 oz (100 g) caster sugar	roughly chopped

To make the *pasta frolla*, sift the flour with the baking powder and mix with the sugar. Place the butter and lard, roughly cut up, in a pan with the wine and heat gently until the fats have almost all melted. Mix with the sifted flour to form a soft dough – you may not need quite all of the liquid, so go carefully. Knead briefly to smooth out, then wrap loosely in a floured cloth and leave to rest for an hour or so.

For the filling, sieve the ricotta, then beat with the milk until creamy. Mix in the sugar and salt.

Take walnut-sized pieces of dough and roll out thinly into a roughly circular shape. Place a generous teaspoon of the sweetened ricotta in the centre of each one and top with a couple of pieces of chocolate. Fold the dough over to cover the ricotta, and press down firmly all around the filling to seal. With a pastry wheel, trim off the excess pastry to form a crescent shape.

Heat a 1-inch- (2.5-cm)-deep layer of oil in a wide frying-pan over a moderate heat. Fry the *Cassatedde* a few at a time until puffed and browned. Drain briefly on kitchen paper, then roll in caster sugar. Eat warm or cold.

Ⓥ

Torta di Mandorle e Ricotta
Almond, Ricotta and Honey Cheesecake

This is a recipe I've had for a long time, based on a baked cheesecake that I ate in a now defunct restaurant in London. It brings together a quartet of ingredients – ricotta, almonds, lemon, honey – that seem quintessentially Sicilian. What makes this version special is that unblanched almonds are used – that is, almonds that are still in their velvety brown skins – so that the baked filling is flecked with brown and has a pure almond-laden flavour.

SERVES 6–8

10 oz (275 g) shortcrust pastry

Filling

3 oz (75 g) unblanched almonds	3 tablespoons caster sugar
1 lb (450 g) ricotta cheese	pinch of salt
3 eggs, separated	finely grated zest of 1 lemon
5 tablespoons honey	juice of ½ lemon

Use the pastry to line a tart tin 2 in (5 cm) deep and about 9 inches (23 cm) in diameter with a removable base. Crimp the edges. Rest in the refrigerator for 30 minutes.

Pre-heat the oven to 375°F (190°C), gas mark 5.

Prick the base of the pastry case, line with foil or greaseproof paper and fill with baking beans. Bake in the oven for 10 minutes. Remove the beans and foil, and return to the oven for 3–5 minutes to dry out. Cool until tepid or cold.

To make the filling, grind the unblanched almonds to a powder. Beat the ricotta until smooth, then beat in the egg yolks, honey, sugar, salt, lemon zest and juice, and the ground almonds. Whisk the egg whites stiffly and fold into the ricotta mixture. Spoon into the pastry case. Bake at 350°F (180°C), gas mark 4, for 30–40 minutes, until just set. Leave to cool in the tin, then chill for 4 hours. Unmould and serve.

Istanbul
TURKEY

Soups, Starters and Meze Dishes

Meat

Side-dishes and Sauces

Desserts

Bread

Istanbul
TURKEY

To be fair, Istanbul is probably not the ideal place to go for a break when you are seven months pregnant. The traffic is horrendous, the smog of pollution hangs over the city in a constant hazy canopy, the noise never abates, except for a blissful period shortly before dawn, soon broken by the wailing of the muezzin from the tower of a nearby mosque. To cap it all, there was a rubbish strike, and street corners were piled high with stinking rotting debris. Just as well that it was the end of October, not high summer.

Perhaps I had expected too much – so many of my friends had returned enraptured with the place – but I was disappointed. I'd imagined a mysterious, beautiful, exotic city, poised at the very limit of Europe, but more Arabian in spirit. That at any rate is true, but to me it seemed that the beauty is limited to the skyline and a few choice sites which in the end bear little relation to the reality of daily life.

Still, Istanbul had its moments, and a fair number of those were connected with food. The famous *Misir Carsisi* (Spice Market) down by the port has become a 'must' on the tourist itinerary, but it hasn't yet lost too much of its spirit. Nestled under the vaulted arches are clusters of small shops, most of them specializing in spices, dried fruits, honeys and sweets or dried meats, with a sprinkling of trinketry and copperware.

At first glance the spice stalls look glorious with glowing heaps of spices in jewelled colours. On closer inspection the choice presented is limited – you have to investigate beyond the frontage to find those things of real interest. On several occasions I was offered saffron at ridiculously low prices, and the stall-holders were most offended when I pointed out that it was heavily adulterated, if indeed the packets contained any saffron at all. More fun were the pots of aphrodisiacs, vile concoctions of herbs, spices and honey, guaranteed to enhance your love life. That bit of hokum I couldn't resist.

But it was the dried-fruit shops that really appealed, with their sacks of delicious Izmir raisins still clinging to the stalk, scented apricots, sticky plump dates, fat figs bursting with seeds, and surreal strings of dried aubergine bells, looking for all the world like outsize black foxgloves. Here too was the place to buy *lokum* (Turkish

Simit-seller in on the streets of Istanbul.

delight) and sweet gelatinous *sucuk*, a type of sausage, but in this instance a sausage of concentrated boiled-down grape juice with nuts running through the centre).

In the end, it was a less showy market that caught my imagination. This was the Wednesday Market, in a residential area of old Istanbul. Spice stalls were well in evidence – less colourful but, when it came down to it, far more interesting with their little packets of sour *sumac*, ground *mahleb* and other unfamiliar spices.

Strings of women clad in black from head to foot wove their way through the crowds, making their weekly purchases from stalls selling enormous cauliflowers and cabbages and yard-long leeks. Here there was a pickled vine-leaf seller, picking his wares from a wooden barrel; there a table laden with three or four different types of aubergine; and over there a mile-high wodge of paper-thin circles of pastry for making *börek*, beside a neat row of jars full of rose-petal jam.

We were glad to escape the city smog, taking a boat up the Bosporus almost as far as the Black Sea. We passed Kanlica, famous for its yoghurt. Though all but

Coffee and Coffee Houses

Coffee is not quite in the demon drink category, being after all a largely approved and accepted stimulant. But stimulant it definitely is. As a drink it can bring life to the most befuddled of brains, its only real vice being the gift of sleeplessness. But its appearance in the Islamic world got mixed reactions.

In sixteenth-century Constantinople, today's Istanbul, the distinctly unpleasant grand vizier, Koprulu, power behind the throne of Sultan (Mehmet) Murad 4, felt it necessary to wage a little war against the idle talk and discontent being spread through the city's flourishing coffee houses. Imams complained at the numbers who sat to talk and drink coffee while their mosques became increasingly empty. Koprulu thought that the threat to order was too great and proceeded to arrest and even torture coffee-house proprietors, driving the coffee drinker underground. For anyone foolish enough to be arrested twice, the punishment was absurdly brutal. The culprit would be sewn up in a leather bag and tossed into the Bosporus to drown.

Today, coffee drinking in the Islamic world, as in Europe, has become a means of relaxing away from the home, a social event, where conversation flows along with the coffee. To this day the coffee houses of Istanbul, although at odds somewhat with hectic city life, are full of a curious mix of people. Now, usually a retired man, the typical coffee-house drinker sits quietly, puffing on his *narghileh* (hubble-bubble pipe, filled, please note, with nothing stronger than tobacco), and is served with cups of tea and coffee throughout his stay there. Women are not welcome, although earnest tourists do persevere.

In Turkey coffee-making remains a respected art. First, the choice of blend is important, which may typically be a mix of strong Mocha beans from Yemen, with milder beans, perhaps from Brazil. The technique of making Turkish coffee is somewhat different from Western methods, giving a stronger, generally sweetened cup of dark milkless brew. To make one you will need an *ibrik*, a small long-handled pot, which you can buy with a little research, filled with some freshly, very finely ground coffee, a little sugar to taste and a small cupful of water (filtered if possible). Heat the water with the sugar, add the grounds and bring to the boil three times, taking it off the heat just as it comes to the boil. Let the grounds settle, and serve, preferably in small porcelain coffee cups. Try an added cardamom pod for a touch of authenticity, or even a little cinnamon. Don't drink this if you're trying to go to sleep!

deserted at this time of year, during the summer months every café is packed with Istanbulites, who have come for the cool breezes and to eat pots of the soothing, slippery, white curds.

Our first stop was a little further along at Anadolu Kavagi, another summer escape, peppered with waterfront fish restaurants offering fried mussels with garlicky sauce, skewers of swordfish or small sardines, grilled bonito and bluefish fillet, not to mention the fishy find of the trip, as far as William was concerned, thick steaks of firm, sweet-fleshed spiny turbot. Later, as we crossed to the opposite bank of the Bosporus, we couldn't miss the ruins of the castle that hung over the little harbour, guarding the entrance to the Black Sea, where much of that fish had been caught.

We docked in Sariyer, a small prosperous town, refuge from the chaos of Istanbul for many a well-heeled family. Nesrin and Ferruh Ilter, he an ex-mayor of Istanbul and now governmental advisor, fit the bill, with a compact but elegant flat looking straight out over the water. Nesrin is a dedicated cook and generous hostess, and it is impossible to spend even half an hour in her home without being plied with a stream of delicious bits and pieces to nibble at.

Sariyer itself is full of interesting food shops. The Sariyer *Karaköy Börekcisi* is commonly known as the musical *börek* shop. *Börek* (flaky savoury pastries) come in coils, in shorter smaller lengths, or in squares, filled with meat or cheese. The joy of this shop is not only the excellent *börek* themselves, but the way in which they are cut up. The man at the counter wields his cleaver to a syncopated beat, banging out popular rhythms as he chops.

On opposite corners of a small square stand the Sariyer *Baklavacisi* and the Sariyer *Muhallebicisi*, sister shops that do a roaring afternoon trade. There's an impressive array of syrup-soaked pastries in the *Baklavacisi*, and the display on the other side of the road seems meagre in comparison – dish after dish of white or caramel-brown glunk. This is *muhallebi*, milk and chicken-breast pudding, which may sound peculiar, but is actually a considerable delicacy, which we both took quite a shine to. The *Muhallebicisi* also sells other deserts and savouries based on dairy products, but it is the chicken-breast pudding that pulls in the crowds, day in day out.

With appetites mildly dampened by a spot of afternoon indulgence, we returned to the Ilters' flat, where preparations for a slap-up supper were in full swing. Heaven knows how we made it through the vast array of food that eventually appeared before us, but I dare say greed and curiosity played their part. I'd been surprised that so little in the way of spices and herbs were used in the kitchens around Istanbul, but Nesrin's spread needed no embellishment.

Ⓥ

Kırmızı Mercimek Çorbası
Red Lentil and Bulgur Soup

When we first arrived at Nesrin Ilter's flat, we sat down for a quick coffee and started talking food – a dangerous subject, for within minutes we were being given tastes of this and that, among them this lentil and bulgur soup, made slightly out of the ordinary by the last-minute addition of lemon juice. Nesrin's version was also enriched with a little cream, but when I made it at home, I decided that I preferred the soup without.

Bulgur is cracked wheat, now sold by some enterprising supermarkets here, but failing that by most wholefood shops. It may also be labelled 'burgul'.

SERVES 4–6

1 large onion, finely chopped
1½ oz (40 g) butter
6 oz (175 g) red lentils
4 oz (100 g) bulgur (cracked wheat)
2½ pints (1.5 litres) chicken, meat or
    vegetable stock

2 tablespoons tomato purée
generous pinch of ground chilli
½ teaspoon dried mint
½ teaspoon ground cumin
salt and pepper
3–4 tablespoons lemon juice

Cook the onion in the butter in a large pan until tender and golden. Add all the remaining ingredients except the lemon juice. Bring to the boil, then simmer gently, covered, until the lentils have dissolved to a mush – around 30 minutes, though this varies from one batch of lentils to another. Stir occasionally to prevent catching. Stir in the lemon juice – the soup should have a lightly sour flavour, but it shouldn't be overwhelming. Adjust the seasoning and serve.

Two Simple Yoghurt Dishes

Yoghurt plays an important part in the Turkish diet, as a sauce, as a dip, or just as a snack. A saucer of thick strained yoghurt often arrives as part of the meze, *sometimes plain, sometimes embellished as in the two recipes that follow.*

Dere Ertlu Süzme Yogurt
Yoghurt with Dill

SERVES 4

5 fl oz (150 ml) Greek-style yoghurt
2–3 tablespoons chopped fresh dill
salt

Mix the yoghurt with the dill and add salt to taste.

Cacık
Yoghurt with Cucumber and Garlic

SERVES 4

½ cucumber, peeled and finely diced
1 tablespoon white wine vinegar
salt

5 fl oz (150 ml) Greek-style yoghurt
1 clove garlic, crushed
1 tablespoon chopped fresh mint
(optional)

Spread the cucumber in a colander, sprinkle with the vinegar and a little salt, then leave to drain for 1 hour. Pat dry with kitchen paper or a clean tea-towel. Mix with the yoghurt and garlic. If you wish, stir in 1 tablespoon mint. Taste and add salt if needed.

Ⓥ

Ezme
Fine-chopped Tomato Salad

Ezme *sits somewhere between a salad, a relish and a kind of a dip. Really it belongs with the* meze *as part of the first course, accompanied by plenty of warm pitta bread, but you could just as well serve it alongside grilled kebabs or fish.*

The important thing is to get all the ingredients chopped so finely that they form a lumpy purée, without dissolving totally into each other. Those with a taste for fire might like to up the quantity of chilli.

SERVES 6–8

1 lb (450 g) ripe tomatoes, skinned, seeded and chopped
¼ cucumber, peeled and chopped
salt
1 green pepper, seeded and chopped
3 spring onions, chopped
1 clove garlic, chopped

½ tablespoon dried mint
1 tablespoon tomato purée
generous pinch of ground chilli
¼ teaspoon caster sugar
2 tablespoons olive oil
1 tablespoon white wine vinegar

Place the tomatoes and cucumber in a colander, sprinkle lightly with salt and leave to drain for at least 30 minutes. Mix with the other vegetables and garlic, and chop very, very finely, until you have a coarse lumpy purée. Stir in the remaining ingredients, taste and adjust the seasoning.

The salad can also be made in a processor, but take care not to process to a mush. Process the vegetables and garlic in very short bursts until very finely chopped and mix with the remaining ingredients in a clean bowl.

Ⓥ
Fasulye Piyazı
White Bean Salad

Though you could make a quick version of this salad with tinned haricot or cannellini beans, the texture of home-cooked ones is usually better, as long as you don't overboil them to a mush. The proportions of beans to other ingredients can be varied at will, though the beans should always predominate.

SERVES 6

6 oz (175 g) haricot beans, soaked in
   water overnight and drained
juice of ½ lemon
6 tablespoons olive oil
salt and pepper

1 red onion, chopped
1 large tomato, skinned, seeded and diced
2 tablespoons finely chopped fresh parsley
8 black olives
2 hard-boiled eggs, quartered

Put the beans into a pan with water to cover generously. Bring to the boil, boil hard for 10 minutes, then reduce the heat and simmer until very tender – probably 40 minutes – 1 hour, but this depends on their age, so try one every 5 minutes or so towards the end of the cooking time. Drain well and mix immediately with about two-thirds of the lemon juice and olive oil, and season with salt and pepper. Leave to cool.

Sprinkle the onion lightly with salt in a bowl and leave for 10 minutes. Rub well, and then rinse. Drain thoroughly. Mix with the beans, tomato and parsley and the rest of the lemon juice and olive oil as required. Spoon into a serving dish and garnish with the olives and eggs.

Ⓥ
Zeytinyaglı Taze Fasulye
Runner Beans in Olive Oil

Beans stewed in olive oil are something we came across frequently, and Nesrin offered to show me how they are cooked. It's a blissfully simple recipe – everything goes into the pot, quickly layered up without ceremony, and then the whole lot is left to simmer very gently, without even the need for any stirring. In October a type of runner bean is the hot favourite, though earlier in the year smaller green beans are given the same treatment.

SERVES 4–6

1 lb (450 g) runner or large French beans, topped and tailed
1 onion, sliced
1 large tomato weighing about 8 oz (225 g), skinned and sliced

½ tablespoon sugar
salt and pepper
3 fl oz (85 ml) olive oil

Snap the beans in half. Cover the base of a large pan with half the onion slices, then place half the tomato slices on top. Pile in the beans, then cover with the remaining onion and tomato. Sprinkle with sugar, salt and pepper and pour over the olive oil. Add enough water to come about two-thirds of the way up the beans. Bring to a gentle simmer, then cover and cook gently for 50 minutes–1 hour without stirring. Spoon into a serving dish with some of the juice (don't use it all, or the beans will be drowned in it) and leave to cool. Serve cold.

Ⓥ
Sigara Böregi
Cigar Börek

Cigar Börek *are the easiest of the many forms of* börek *(savoury pastries) to make at home, taking their name from their shape. Fillings can vary, but feta cheese and herbs is the one we came across most frequently. Be warned: Cigar* Börek *are very more-ish, and though two dozen may sound like a fair number, they'll soon be snapped up and eaten.*

MAKES 22–24

About 6 sheets filo pastry
2 oz (55 g) unsalted butter, melted

Filling

8 oz (225 g) feta cheese, crumbled
1 egg, lightly beaten
2 tablespoons finely chopped fresh parsley
2 tablespoons finely chopped fresh dill

Preheat the oven to 375°F (190°C), gas mark 5.

To make the filling, mash the cheese and beat with the egg to form a cream. Stir in the herbs. Whatever you do, don't add any salt, as feta is already quite salty enough.

Cut the filo into strips about 4 × 10 inches (10 × 25 cm) or a close approximation that fits the size of your filo sheets. Keep the filo from drying out while you work by covering first with a sheet of greaseproof paper and then with a tea-towel wrung out in cold water.

Take the first strip of filo, brush with butter, then place a generous teaspoon of the filling close to one of the short ends, shaping it into a small sausage parallel to the edge. Flip over the long sides to cover the ends of the filling, then roll up neatly to form a little cigar shape. Repeat with the remaining filling until used up.

Lay the *börek* on greased baking sheets and brush with melted butter. (They can be stored in the refrigerator for up to 8 hours at this stage, or frozen.) Bake for 10–15 minutes, until golden-brown. Serve hot or warm, and don't worry if a little filling oozes out here or there: just tidy it away and no one will be any the wiser.

Midye Tavası
Fried Mussels with Garlic and Walnut Sauce

I looked longingly at the frying mussels when we were at Anadolu Kavagi, on the banks of the Bosporus, but, being pregnant, I thought it best to resist temptation, just in case. Nonetheless I did pay careful attention to their preparation, and noticed the relish with which those around me were downing them.

Back at home, I tried making them for myself and was delighted with the results. As long as the frying oil is good and hot, the mussels don't toughen or dry out as I had thought they might. And the combination of sweet hot mussels with the garlicky walnut sauce is stunning.

S E R V E S 4–6 as a first course

2 lb (900 g) mussels
seasoned flour
1–2 eggs, lightly beaten
sunflower oil for frying
Garlic and Walnut Sauce (see p.121)
to serve

Scrub the mussels well, scraping off the beards and small barnacles. Rinse thoroughly in several changes of water. Discard any that refuse to close when tapped sharply against a work surface, or that feel abnormally heavy (these are likely to be filled with mud and grit). Heat a ½-inch (1-cm) depth of water in a large wide pan until boiling. Add the mussels, cover tightly and shake over a high heat for a few minutes until they have opened. Discard any mussels that steadfastly refuse to open. Take the mussels (the orange meat) out of their shells and reserve them.

To finish, thread the mussels on to wooden skewers that have been pre-soaked in water for 30 minutes. Allow about 6 mussels per skewer and don't pack them too tightly. Coat each skewerful first in seasoned flour, then in beaten egg, and finally in flour again, making sure that it is thoroughly coated each time. Fry in hot oil, turning occasionally with tongs, until golden-brown. Drain briefly on kitchen paper. Serve immediately with Garlic and Walnut Sauce.

ⓥ

Tarator
Garlic and Walnut Sauce

Tarator sauce is a wonderful concoction, pungent and rich, yet marrying well with all kinds of food, particularly fish. It should have the consistency of relaxed mayonnaise, not too thick and not too sloppy either. I happen to like it best made with walnuts, but pine nuts are good too. Use up any left-overs on hot boiled vegetables – delicious.

SERVES 6–8

2 slices of stale white bread – about 2½ oz (65 g) – crusts removed
3 cloves garlic, crushed
1–2 tablespoons white wine vinegar

2 oz (50 g) walnuts or pine nuts, ground finely
salt
6 tablespoons olive oil

Soak the bread in water for 10 minutes. Drain and gently squeeze out the water.

To make the sauce in a liquidizer or processor, whizz the bread with the garlic, vinegar, nuts and salt until smooth, then gradually drizzle in the olive oil. Taste and adjust the seasoning.

Without a processor, pound the bread with the garlic, nuts and salt in a mortar until you have a smooth paste. Work in the vinegar, then the oil a little at a time. Taste and adjust the seasoning.

OVERLEAF
Top: *Simit* (Sesame Bread Rings) see p. 136. Background: *Patlıcan Kebabı* (Aubergines Stuffed with Lamb) see p. 124. Foreground: *Midye Tavası* (Fried Mussels with Garlic and Walnut Sauce) see p. 120.

Patlıcan Kebabı
Aubergines Stuffed with Lamb

Aubergines are terrifically important in Turkish cuisine, used for all sorts of dishes. Nesrin cooked this dish of aubergines stuffed with a tomatoey lamb filling for us. She uses slender aubergines, thinner than the ones we can buy here.

When I came to make Patlıcan Kebabı *(patlican means 'aubergine', and kebab, you may be surprised to know, means that the dish contains meat – nothing to do with skewers at all), I thought that one of our large aubergines would satisfy two people. Don't you believe it. One person can easily make their way through an entire stuffed aubergine.*

By the way, the lamb filling, which is nothing more than a tomatoey stew, is also very good with Hünkar Begendi, *the aubergine purée on p.125.*

SERVES 4

4 aubergines	4 6-inch (15-cm)-long, spindly, mild,
salt	green chillies or 1 small green pepper,
sunflower oil for frying	seeded and cut into wide strips
1 tomato, thickly sliced	

Filling

1 large onion, chopped	salt and pepper
1 oz (25 g) butter	1 large tomato, weighing around 8 oz
1 lb (450 g) tender lamb (such as leg), cut	(225 g), skinned, seeded and diced
into ¾-inch (2-cm) cubes	2 tablespoons tomato purée
½ teaspoon ground chilli	1 teaspoon sugar

Slice the stems off the aubergines. Take 4 strips of peel off each one, from top to tail, so that it is striped with purple skin and white flesh. Place in a basin, sprinkle over 1 generous tablespoon salt, cover with water and leave for an hour to soak, turning occasionally.

Drain the aubergines and dry. Heat a 1-inch (2.5-cm) depth of sunflower oil in a frying-pan large enough to take all the aubergines (or, if necessary, cook in 2 batches). Fry the aubergines, turning, until browned on all sides and tender (this should take about 15–20 minutes). Drain on kitchen paper. Place in an oiled ovenproof dish and cut a deep slit in each one along its length, without cutting through the ends. Gently ease open to form a pocket for the filling.

Make the filling while the aubergines are soaking. Fry the onion in the butter until tender without browning. Add the lamb, chilli and some pepper and fry, stirring occasionally, for 10 minutes. Add the diced tomato, tomato purée and sugar and cook for a further 5 minutes. Pour in 5 fl oz (150 ml) water, season with salt and simmer, covered, for about 1 hour, until the meat is very tender.

Preheat the oven to 400°F (200°C), gas mark 6.

Fill the aubergines with the meat and pour over any juice that remains in the pan. Place a slice of tomato and a green chilli (or wide strip of green pepper) on top of each one. Bake in the oven for 20 minutes. Serve hot or warm.

Ⓥ

Hünkar Begendi
Sultan's Delight

Here's how the story goes: a sultan, out on a hunt in the forest, got lost. At last he saw a light and made for it, in desperate need of food and shelter. His solicitous host, who had long since eaten his evening meal, sent word to the cook to bring more food. Little remained in the kitchen, apart from some left-overs and a brace of aubergines. The cook, in an inspired moment, came up with this purée of grilled aubergines flavoured with a stub of hard old cheese, topped with a snappily made stew of the left-over meat from his master's supper. The sultan was delighted.

SERVES 4

2 large aubergines weighing about 1½ lb (750 g) in total	15 fl oz (450 ml) milk
1½ oz (40 g) butter	2 oz (450 g) Parmesan cheese, freshly grated
1½ oz (40 g) flour	salt and pepper
	chopped fresh parsley

Grill the aubergines whole, turning frequently, until blackened and blistered all over and soft to the touch. Drop into a plastic bag and leave until cool enough to handle. Cut in half, strip off the skin and chop the flesh roughly. Pile into a colander and leave to drain for 30 minutes. Press to squeeze out the last of the bitter juices.

While the aubergines are draining, melt the butter and stir in the flour. Stir for a few minutes until biscuit-coloured. Off the heat, beat in the milk a little at a time to form a white sauce. Bring back to the boil and simmer for 10 minutes, until thick.

Process the aubergine with the sauce. If you don't have a processor, chop the aubergine finely, then mash as thoroughly as you can before mixing into the sauce. Return to the heat, stir in the cheese, and salt and pepper to taste, and warm through, stirring. Spoon on to a warm serving dish, scatter with parsley and serve with grilled meats, *köfte* or stews (the lamb filling for the *Patlıcan Kebabı* (see p.124) goes very well with this.

Izgara Köfte
Grilled Köfte

Istanbul's Sultanahmet Köfte *Shop, near the Blue Mosque, is reckoned to serve the best* köfte *(minced meat 'balls') in town. People of all classes crowd into the shop at lunchtime to down a quick plate of the famous* köfte. *On the walls there are framed poems proclaiming their glory.*

The ingredients are disarmingly few – minced beef, bread, onion, salt and pepper. The secret, they say, lies in the quality of the meat. Prime cuts from cattle raised in different areas of the country are used. Every morning the different batches of meat are blended carefully to get just the right balance!

You can order a side-salad of lettuce, tomato, cucumber and feta cheese, or of plain white beans; you can tart up your köfte *with a spoonful of yoghurt, or a sprinkling of chilli flakes and oregano, but other than that the formula is set.*

SERVES 4

2 thick slices of day-old white bread, crusts removed
1 lb (450 g) best-quality minced beef or lamb

1 onion, grated or very finely chopped
1 teaspoon ground cumin (optional)
salt and pepper
olive oil

To serve

chilli flakes
dried oregano

Soak the bread in water for 10 minutes. Drain and squeeze dry, then crumble. Mix with the meat, onion, cumin (if using), salt and pepper, then whizz in a processor or pass through a mincer. Knead the mixture with your hands for a few minutes until smooth and cohesive. Divide into 12 portions and roll each one into either a tubby sausage shape or a small rugby ball. Brush with oil and grill for 5–6 minutes until just cooked through, but still slightly pink at heart. Serve with chilli and oregano for those who want to spice them up. A salad of tomato, lettuce and cucumber is a good accompaniment.

Kadınbudu Köfte
Lady's Thigh Köfte

These are the köfte *I like best, fried rather than grilled, and with a very particular texture — so smooth that it is meant to resemble a lady's thigh — given by the rice and the curious mixture of cooked and uncooked minced meat.*

SERVES 4–6

1 lb (450 g) minced lamb or beef
1 onion, finely chopped
1 oz (25 g) butter
1 oz (25 g) uncooked rice
salt and pepper

1 teaspoon ground cinnamon
2 tablespoons finely chopped fresh parsley
3 eggs
seasoned flour
oil for frying

Process the meat in brief bursts until very finely minced. Fry the onion gently in the butter until golden and tender, then add the rice, salt and 8 fl oz (250 ml) water. Cover and simmer gently until all the water is absorbed and the rice is tender.

Meanwhile take half the meat and place it in a dry heavy-based saucepan. Sauté, with no added fat, for about 5 minutes, until the meat's juices have evaporated. Tip it into a bowl with the remaining raw meat. Add the cooked rice and onions, drained if necessary (though it shouldn't be) of any liquid, the cinnamon, parsley, salt, pepper and enough egg to bind (you should need at most 1 egg). Mix, then knead for 5 minutes, until smooth.

Divide into 12 portions. Dampen your hands to prevent sticking, then roll each portion into a ball and flatten to form an oval.

Beat the remaining eggs lightly. Dip the *köfte* into beaten egg, then coat thoroughly in seasoned flour. Fry in oil over a medium heat until browned on both sides. Eat immediately.

Adana Kebabı
Spiced Grilled Meatballs

Adana Kebabı *are made from meat alone – no breadcrumbs to soften the texture – and zipped up with a light sprinkling of spice. Though the ones we ate in Istanbul were good, I prefer to increase the spices, so that their flavour is more distinct without ever being overwhelming.*

SERVES 6

1½ lb (750 g) best-quality minced beef or lamb

1 large onion, grated

3 tablespoons finely chopped fresh parsley

1 teaspoon dried oregano

½ teaspoon ground chilli

1 teaspoon ground cumin

½ teaspoon ground allspice

salt and pepper

1 egg, beaten

olive oil

sliced tomatoes and onions to serve

Mix the meat with the onion, parsley, oregano, spices, salt and pepper. Process together briefly, then scoop into a bowl and knead in enough egg to bind. Keep kneading for about 5 minutes, until the mixture is smooth and sticky.

Divide into 6 portions. Roll each into a fat sausage about 6 inches (15 cm) long, then, using your hand, squidge it around a skewer, pressing firmly, so that the skewer is enclosed in a mincemeat casing. Brush with oil and grill for about 8 – 10 minutes, turning occasionally, until just cooked. Serve with sliced tomatoes and onions.

İç Pilav
Chicken Liver *Pilav*

As Nesrin cooked, I couldn't help noticing two similarities between the cooking of Sicily and Turkey — at least, of this part of the country. Aubergines play an immensely important role in both, and the pairing of pine nuts and currants re-emerged in this recipe.

SERVES 6

10 oz (275 g) medium or long-grain rice
salt and pepper
2 oz (50 g) unsalted butter
1 large onion, chopped
2 oz (50 g) pine nuts
6 oz (175 g) chicken livers, chopped

1 pint (600 ml) hot chicken stock
1 heaped teaspoon ground cinnamon
1 teaspoon ground allspice
1 teaspoon caster sugar
2 oz (50 g) currants
3 tablespoons chopped fresh dill

Pour hot water over the rice, stir in 1 heaped teaspoon salt and leave until cold. Drain and rinse thoroughly. Leave in a sieve to finish draining.

Melt the butter in a large saucepan, and add the onion and pine nuts. Cook until the onion is lightly browned. Add the chicken livers, salt and pepper and cook, stirring, for 2 minutes. Now add the rice and continue to stir for about 4 minutes. Pour in the hot stock and stir in the spices, sugar and currants, and more salt and pepper. Bring to a simmer, reduce the heat and cover tightly. Leave to cook for 15–20 minutes, without stirring, until the rice is just done and all the liquid is absorbed. Only add more stock (or water) if absolutely necessary. Stir in the dill, turn off the heat, cover again and leave to stand for a final 5 minutes.

Mantı
Tiny Meat Dumplings with Yoghurt and Garlic Sauce

While Nesrin cooked the rest of the supper, she brought in a specialist to make the Mantı. *Makbule Ozkan comes from Cappodocia, and travelled to Sariyer with her husband many years ago in search of work. Now she is a professional freelance cook, working in houses all around Sariyer.*

Mantı, *minuscule meat dumplings, are said to have originated in Mongolia, and to be honest they are not an undertaking for anyone with a busy schedule. Makbule, who works at the speed of light, took a good three-quarters of an hour to make enough for six of us.*

For the novice, Mantı *demand untold reservoirs of patience . . . unless you do as I did when I came to make them. I cheated: I doubled their size – far less fiddly and time-consuming. If you do not wish to cheat, I would strongly urge you to rope in a helper, preferably a good friend to whom you can chat as you pinch and fold the dough.*

The good news is that the Mantı *can be prepared several hours in advance, and stored in the refrigerator, covered with a tea-towel (not cling film or foil, which will make them damp and sweaty), or even frozen.*

SERVES 4

Dough

8 oz (225 g) strong plain flour	1 egg
¼ teaspoon salt	

Filling

6 oz (175 g) minced lamb or beef	1 tablespoon very finely chopped fresh
¼ onion, grated	parsley
	salt and pepper

To cook and serve

2 pints (1.2 litres) good stock	Yoghurt and Garlic Sauce (see p.131)
3 oz (75 g) butter	dried mint
1 heaped teaspoon ground chilli	*sumac*

To make the dough, sift the flour with the salt. Make a well in the centre and add the egg and a little water. Mix, gradually adding more water as needed, until you have a soft dough. Knead for 10 minutes until satin-smooth and elastic. Divide into 6 portions, cover with a damp tea-towel and leave to rest for 30 minutes.

Meanwhile make the filling. If you have a processor, whizz all the ingredients together. Otherwise mix by hand, kneading thoroughly until you have a cohesive mass.

Roll out each portion of dough one at a time, using a thin wooden rolling pin. The dough should be as thin as you can get it without tearing – no more than $\frac{1}{8}$ inch (3 mm) at most. Keep the rest of the dough covered while you work so that it doesn't dry out. With a sharp knife cut the rolled dough into 1-inch (2.5-cm) squares (if you are very patient and nimble-fingered) or 2-inch (5-cm) squares (if you don't have all day to fiddle about). Working quickly so that the dough doesn't dry too much, place a blob of filling – a very small one for small squares, about ¼ teaspoon for larger squares – in the centre of each piece of dough. Bring the 4 corners up to meet over each blob of filling, pinching them together. Pinch the edges quickly together so that you form a little bag shape, like a mitred cap. Keep going until all the dough is used up. Chill for 30 minutes, uncovered, in the refrigerator.

To cook, bring the stock to the boil in a wide shallow pan. Tip in half the dumplings and poach for 6 minutes or so if small, 10–12 minutes if large. Scoop out into a warm serving dish, spoon over a little of the stock to keep moist, then cover loosely and keep warm in the oven while you poach the remaining dumplings.

Make the chilli butter while they cook. Melt the butter in a frying-pan and add the chilli. Stir over a very low heat for 4–5 minutes.

To serve, spoon over about half the yoghurt sauce, then drizzle over a little of the red chilli butter and sprinkle with a trail of dried mint. Serve the remaining yoghurt sauce, chilli butter, mint and *sumac* (if you have it) separately.

Ⓥ

Sarımsaklı Yogurt
Yoghurt and Garlic Sauce

This is the sauce to serve with Mantı *(p.130), though unlike the dumplings it can be made in the twinkling of an eye. But don't reserve it just for* Mantı. *Try it with grilled meats of all kinds, or as an accompaniment to stuffed vegetables.*

SERVES 4–6

12 oz (350 g) Greek-style yoghurt
3 cloves garlic, crushed
salt

Beat all the ingredients together with 2 tablespoons water. Taste and adjust the seasoning.

ⓥ
Baklava
Syrup and Nut Pastry

The pastry room upstairs at the Gullouglu Baklava Bakery is an amazing sight. In a haze of white flour a dozen men are pulling and stretching out the paper-thin dough. They look like ghosts, covered from head to foot in a fine white dusting of flour. Even the telephone high on the wall looks bizarre – something from a theatrical set perhaps? It was only when I emerged back on to the streets that I suddenly looked down and realized that I too had metamorphosed into a ghostly figure.

A quick dust down and it was round to the shop to buy a selection of Baklava, *those sticky nut-filled pastries with their many layers of crisp buttery filo pastry.*

Home-baked Baklava *are never quite the same as really good professional ones, made by skilled bakers, but they are a pleasure to make for all that. Adjusting the cooking time and temperature to suit your oven is important – the idea is to make sure that every layer of pastry is crisp through to the heart. Treat my instructions as guidelines, and keep an eye on the* Baklava *as they cook. If they seem to be browning far too fast, reduce the temperature slightly and/or cover loosely with foil.*

SERVES 12

1 lb (450 g) filo pastry
4 oz (100 g) unsalted butter, melted

Nut filling

12 oz (350 g) walnuts or pistachios
   (or a mixture of the two), coarsely
   ground or *very* finely chopped
1 tablespoon ground cinnamon

Syrup

10 oz (275 g) granulated sugar
juice of 1 lemon

Preheat the oven to 350°F (180°C), gas mark 4.

To prevent the filo drying out, cover it first with a sheet of greaseproof paper then with a tea-towel wrung out in cold water. Brush a 13 × 10 inch (33 × 25 cm) baking dish with a little of the butter. Brush half the sheets of filo pastry with butter and lay in the baking dish, one on top of the other. Spread over the filling ingredients, then cover with the remaining pastry sheets, again buttering each one before laying it down.

Using a sharp knife, tuck the edges down neatly round the sides. Brush with the remaining butter. Using a sharp knife, cut into diamonds. Bake in the oven for 25 minutes, then reduce the heat to 300°F (150°C), gas mark 2, and bake for a further 30 minutes.

While the *Baklava* is cooking, put the sugar for the syrup into a pan with 10 fl oz (300 ml) water and the lemon juice. Stir over a medium heat until the sugar has dissolved, Bring to the boil and simmer for 5 minutes. Cool. As soon as the *Baklava* comes out of the oven, pour over the syrup, then leave to cool completely.

Ⓥ

İmik Helvası
Semolina Pudding

The one pudding on offer at the Sultanahmet Köfte *Shop is* İrmik Helvası. *To translate it as 'semolina pudding' is selling it short. There is no resemblance to the gluey stuff you may well have suffered in your childhood. This is a gem, though it doesn't look too remarkable. The semolina is slowly fried in lots of butter until toasty brown, then boiled up in a milky cinnamon syrup. The* helvası *can be eaten hot, but I think it's far nicer cold, which is how it comes at the* köfte *shop. There they leave it to set in a giant metal pudding basin. Shortly before the lunchtime rush floods in they turn it — a huge tan dome — out on to a board and shear slices from it as the orders come. Within a few hours nothing but the odd crumb remains.*

SERVES 8–10

10 oz (275 g) caster sugar	6 oz (175 g) unsalted butter
1¼ pints (750 ml) milk	9 oz (250 g) semolina
1 cinnamon stick	5 oz (150 g) pine nuts

Put the sugar, milk and cinnamon stick in a large pan and stir over a medium heat until the sugar has dissolved. Bring to the boil, then reduce the heat and simmer gently for 5 minutes.

Melt the butter in a wide deep frying-pan and add the semolina and pine nuts. Fry gently, stirring continuously, until the semolina and nuts are a deep tan colour — about 10 minutes. Watch over it and stir conscientiously towards the end, as it can burn easily if left to its own devices. Draw off the heat and, at arm's length, pour the hot milk syrup slowly into the semolina. Be careful, as it will spit and sizzle angrily. Return to the heat, keeping it low, and stir until all the liquid has been absorbed but the semolina is still moist. It can be served hot at this stage.

Alternatively scoop into a greased bowl and smooth down. Leave to cool and turn out. Serve thinly sliced.

ⓥ

Revani
Lemon Syrup Cake

Semolina again, but cast in a different role. In Revani, *it serves to give a pleasingly grainy texture to the soft crumb of the syrup-soaked cake. This is similar to the one that Nesrin cooked for us, but I've cut down on the syrup, making it a little less sweet and sticky.*

Nonetheless serve the Revani *as a pudding rather than a teatime cake, accompanied by thick Greek-style yoghurt, clotted cream or whipped cream, and perhaps some soft fruit such as raspberries.*

SERVES 6

4 oz (100 g) self-raising flour
pinch of salt
1 level teaspoon baking powder
4 oz (100 g) fine semolina

3 eggs
4 oz (100 g) caster sugar
2 oz (50 g) butter, melted and cooled
finely grated zest of ½ lemon

Syrup

8 oz (225 g) caster sugar
juice of lemon

Preheat the oven to 350°F (180°C), gas mark 4.

Sift the flour with the salt and baking powder. Mix with the semolina. Whisk the eggs with the sugar until pale, light and fluffy. Fold in the flour and semolina mixture, the melted butter and lemon zest. Pour into a well-greased 7-inch (18-cm) square cake tin and bake in the oven for 25–30 minutes, until golden-brown and firm to the touch.

While the cake is cooking, put the syrup ingredients into a pan with 8 fl oz (250 ml) water and stir over a medium heat until the sugar has completely dissolved. Bring to the boil and simmer for 1 minute, then draw off the heat. As soon as the *Revani* comes out of the oven, make a few holes in it with a skewer and pour over the syrup. Leave it to cool and suck in the syrup. It should stand for at least 2 hours before you eat it (it will keep, covered, for at least 3 days). Serve cold, cut into squares.

Ⓥ Ayva Tatlısı
Quince Pudding

I made a bee-line for these poached quinces when I saw a tray of them out at Anadolu Kavagi. Very sweet, it's true, but with such a wonderful flavour. There they served them with a generous scoop of kaymak, *the heavenly rich 'clotted' sheep's milk cream, so thick that you can cut it with a knife. Clotted cream is the best alternative here, but failing that you might try strained Greek yoghurt, or whipped double cream.*

Quinces, though a rarity here, are sometimes available in the autumn from Greek and Turkish food stores.

SERVES 8

2 large or 4 small ripe quinces weighing
    about 2 – 2½ lb (900 g – 1.25 kg) in
    total
1 lb (450 g) caster sugar
clotted cream to serve

Peel the quinces, cut in quarters if large, half if small and scoop out the cores. Take a large square of muslin and tie the cores and peel in it. Place the quinces and muslin parcel in a pan, dredge over the sugar and cover with water. Simmer gently for 1 hour, until the quinces are tender, turning them occasionally as the liquid level drops. Lift them out with a slotted spoon into a serving dish. Boil the syrup (still with the muslin bag in it) until thick and syrupy. Pour over the quinces and leave to cool. Serve with clotted cream.

⒱

Simit

Sesame Bread Rings (Turkish Bagels)

There are Simit-sellers on every street corner in Istanbul, sometimes several clustered together. They may grab their Simits out of a glass-fronted trolley, or tote them around piled up, one on top of another, on a round tray balanced on the head.

Simit are sesame-encrusted Turkish bagels with a lovely chewy crust and a soft white interior that carries a hint of sweetness. Sometimes I've come across them here, but they are by no means commonplace. Still, they are great fun to make, as long as you have a few hours spare to play. What makes the crust chewy is a quick dunking in boiling water before they go into the oven to be cooked properly.

MAKES 6

I oz (25 g) fresh yeast or ½ oz (15 g) dried yeast	2 oz (50 g) butter, melted and cooled until tepid
I teaspoon sugar	I egg yolk
I lb (450 g) strong white flour	about I oz (25 g) sesame seeds
I teaspoon salt	

Cream the yeast and sugar with 5 fl oz (150 ml) warm water. Leave in a warm place for 5–10 minutes, until foaming. Sift the flour with the salt and make a well in the centre. Pour in the yeast mixture and the butter. Mix, gradually drawing in the flour, to form a soft, slightly sticky dough – if necessary, add a little more warm water. Knead for 10 minutes, until you have smooth elastic dough. Dust with flour, cover with a cloth and leave to rise in a warm place until doubled in bulk – about 1 hour.

Punch down and knead again for 5 minutes. Divide into 6 portions and roll each one out to form a thin sausage about 16 inches (40 cm) long. Dampen the ends with water and pinch together to form a ring. Lay on a floured tray and leave to rise for 15 minutes or so in a warm place.

Preheat the oven to 425°F (220°C), gas mark 7.

Bring a large pan of water to the boil. One at a time, drop the *simit* into the water, boil for 1 minute, then remove and drain on a clean towel. Lay on a floured baking sheet. Beat the egg yolk with 1 tablespoon water and brush over the boiled *simit*. Sprinkle heavily with sesame seeds, and bake in the oven for 15–20 minutes until well browned. Cool on a wire rack.

If you wish, you can omit the boiling, but they won't have such a delicious chewy crust.

Kalocsa
HUNGARY

Kalocsa
HUNGARY

By mid-September, according to our guide book, all the fields around Kalocsa would be aflame with paprika. It went on at some lyrical length about this extraordinary sight. As we drove closer and closer to the town, over the endlessly flat plain, the great Hungarian *puszta*, we began to wonder where all these flaming fields had gone to. Had we missed the harvest? Was it a figment of the author's imagination? Should we give up and head back to Budapest?

There was a slightly reassuring poster in the main square. It read: 'Paprika something or other', but the rest we couldn't understand (we'd tried to learn a few words of Hungarian before we came, but I'm afraid we'd given up in utter confusion). Persistent enquiry finally revealed that there was to be a procession to celebrate the harvest at the end of the week. The time and exact route of this procession were both unknown quantities, even in the tourist office, but at least we knew we hadn't come all that way for nothing.

As it turned out, we needn't have worried at all. Taken in hand by our new friend Sarolta Schutz, a local English teacher, we were soon plunged into the world of paprika. The season was a week or two late that year – an over-dry hot summer had slowed down growth – and it was just getting into its stride when we arrived. The author of our guide book was obviously a man prone to exaggeration. The paprika fields are not as widespread as he suggested, but when you do come across them, they fairly take your breath away: huge, huge fields of startling green and red, stretching out into the distance as far as the eye can see.

They get through a lot of paprika down here. We were told that the consumption in this area is twice the national average – somewhere around 2 kg (over 4 lb!) per person per year, as opposed to a mere 1 kg (2¼ lb) elsewhere. Few people buy it ready-milled, preferring instead to grow and dry their own. Once our eyes became attuned to the sight, we soon began to notice small patches of paprika all over the place, in gardens as well as in odd corners of fields.

Vera and Andras Papp both trained as agricultural engineers and used to work in a state farm. After the collapse of communism, the farm was closed down and they lost their jobs and home. They had little choice but to move in with Vera's

Paprika

Some five hundred years ago, a mere nano-moment in terms of world history, the paprika plant was completely unknown in Europe, or indeed anywhere but in its homeland of South and Central America. The spice, Paprika, comes from a plant that we may know otherwise as chilli, red pepper, capsicum or pimiento, that occasionally fiery relation to the tomato. It is a plant that has shown an extraordinary ability to appear almost everywhere on the globe within a remarkably short space of time, in places as far apart as New Guinea and Hungary.

The very best paprika is sold under the teasingly old-fashioned label of Kalocsa Gold and rarely finds its way outside Hungary. It's a well-kept secret, and remains so by the simple fact that there is seldom an excess of supply. Although much paprika is dried and milled at home, it has become an important local industry, and during a visit to a nearby factory we began to unravel the intricacies of the various categories. In the factory the paprika is dried in a machine, but the best grades are stone-ground, which gives a more consistent grain size. The milling process is important, and must be carefully controlled. Once the pods are picked from their stalks, everything is milled together, seeds included, as these give the paprika a richer colour and act as an anti-oxidant. There are six grades of paprika, from the very best Kalocsa Aranya (Kalocsa Gold) to Különleges (Special Grade), Csemege (Delicatessen), Édesnemes (Noble Sweet), Félédes (Half-sweet) and Rózsa (Rose). Complicated? These categories are quite well understood in Hungary, but incomprehensible outside it, though each has an accepted difference in quality. There is, on top of all this, one more important distinction: that between hotness and sweetness. If the paprika has the word *csipos* printed on the container, it is hot. However, don't panic. It's not as hot as chilli pepper, and the Hungarian taste is for a sweeter rounder flavour.

The difference in actual taste between the various types of paprika is quite remarkable, and new kinds are being continually developed. As Hungary begins to look westwards, we may start to see a little more of its finest crop appearing in our shops. If the mood takes you, don't hesitate to buy some, set up a cauldron in the garden, open a bottle of *palinka* or something similar and settle down to a good old Magyar evening strumming the balalaika on horseback. Good luck with the neighbours.

Picking paprika in Kalocsa.

mother, in her small house in Kalocsa. Eventually Andras found work as a salesman, but the salary is barely enough to survive on now that they have a young child.

The courtyard of the house where they live is typical of many in the area. Stepping from the dusty back street through the gate in the high wall, I suddenly found myself in a microscopic jam-packed market-garden-cum-orchard-cum-farmyard.

The Papps grow their own quinces, plums, apples, figs, gooseberries, grapes, kohlrabi, carrots, tomatoes, cabbage, spinach, chard, cauliflower, potatoes and even tobacco. They have four types of paprika (which just means pepper, as in green or red capsicum): the long, tapering, mild type that is dried and ground to make the spice; small and large hot cherry peppers; and, biggest of them all, the Hungarian wax pepper, a cone-shaped pale green sweet pepper like a flavourful version of our own green bell pepper. Livestock includes five goats, a cackle of hens, dozens of rabbits and two fat pigs. In the store-cupboard there are rows of preserves for the winter months. Bottled fruit, jams, syrups, cordials and pickled vegetables abound and, hanging from the ceiling, smoked hams and dried salamis.

Lajos Perity, another friend of Sarolta's, is a horse-dealer, but when harvest-time comes, he and his wife Anna are out in the fields picking along with the rest. It is back-breaking work, hot and sweaty in the sunshine, chilly and cold when it clouds over.

Everyone looks forward to lunch, cooked in the fields in a big cauldron. Outdoor cooking seems to be commonplace here – the requisite cauldrons are sold very cheaply at the Kalocsa market – and you can bet that the cauldron will be filled either with a substantial soup, probably *gulyás*, or a stew, in which case it's some form of *pörkölt*. The difference between the two is the amount of added liquid. Any meat can be used, but the real essentials are lots of paprika and lengthy simmering.

Lunch is a merry affair, eaten standing up around the back of a truck which forms a makeshift table. There are salad pickles – almost as ubiquitous as paprika – plenty of bread, lots of wine from the Perity's own grapes, and sticky cakes to finish.

The cauldrons came out again a few days later when another of Sarolta's friends, Jozsef Fulep, took William off to gallop across the plains in true Magyar fashion. Wearing his full finery Jozsef looked splendid as he sped across the wide flat lands.

Jozsef is a sheep-farmer. He shares the care of his 800 sheep with his two sons, herding them across the *puszta*. Lamb is an expensive meat in Hungary, so this is a good way to earn a living. Jozsef's wife Ilona was left behind in the middle of a field to cook a lamb *pörkölt*, considered a great treat, while the rest of the group galloped off. I gather that the party was a considerable success, with vast quantities of rough red wine and strong *palinka*, *the* Hungarian spirit, to wash down the *pörkölt*.

The day of the paprika procession finally dawned and precise details still seemed to be vague. We hung around the main square in the early afternoon, with practically no one else in sight. We'd just about given up hope when a coach pulled up and disgorged a crowd of youngsters, carrying musical instruments. They disappeared into the hotel, emerging ten minutes later togged up in traditional costume.

With absolutely no preamble they began to play and dance, and suddenly a small crowd gathered from nowhere. I nearly jumped a mile high when the first horseman hurtled into the square, cracking his whip here and there, handsome and dramatic and quite unexpected. The rest of the 'procession' followed swiftly, painted carts filled with pretty girls, and another dozen men on horseback. Totally anarchic and unco-ordinated, or so it seemed, they wheeled round, fiercely and proudly, while the girls danced between the stamping stallions. As quickly as they arrived, they left, and the square emptied of bystanders. Time to go home.

László Csirkegulyása
László's Chicken Goulash

László, a friend of the Peritys, is designated chief cook while the rest of the clan do the seriously hard work, picking the paprika out in the fields. The day we were there, he made both a chicken gulyás, *and a beef* pörkölt *to stoke them up at lunchtime.*

To make the soup more filling he adds postage-stamp squares of noodles right at the end. These can be replaced by small soup pasta, broken up strips of tagliatelle or lasagne, or, more authentically perhaps, by little egg dumplings (see p.147).

SERVES 8

2 tablespoons lard
1 large onion, chopped
2 large carrots, diced
1 celeriac root, diced
1 large boiling chicken, cut into 8 pieces
   (with liver and heart if possible)
1 small bunch of parsley
1½ heaped tablespoons paprika
1 teaspoon caraway seeds
2 bay leaves
1 clove garlic

1 wax pepper or green pepper, seeded
   and roughly sliced
1 hot cherry pepper or dried red chilli
   (optional)
8 oz (225 g) tomatoes, skinned and
   roughly chopped
1 tablespoon tomato purée
salt and pepper
2 large potatoes, peeled and cut into
   1-inch (2.5-cm) cubes
4 oz (100 g) noodles, broken into small
   pieces

Melt the lard in a large pan and add the onion. Cook over a gentle heat until translucent. Now add the carrots and celeriac and cook and stir for about 2 minutes. Next comes the chicken: add it to the pan and let it cook gently, stirring occasionally for 5–10 minutes – it's not particularly meant to brown, though if it does lightly, that's fine.

Add the parsley, paprika, caraway, bay leaves and garlic. Stir well, then pop in the green pepper, whole cherry pepper or dried chilli (if using), tomatoes and tomato purée. Season with salt and pepper, and pour in enough water to cover generously. Bring to the boil and simmer, half-covered, for about 1 hour. Taste occasionally, and if it is getting too chilli-hot for your liking, fish out the cherry pepper or chilli.

Add the diced potato and a little more water if needed (remember: this is a soup, not a stew) and simmer for a further 10 minutes. Add the noodles, and then continue simmering for a final 10 minutes or so. Taste and adjust the seasoning.

László Marhagulyása
László's Beef Goulash

Make as for Chicken Goulash, replacing the chicken with 2 lb (900 g) stewing beef, cut into ¾-inch (2-cm) cubes. Simmer for 2 hours before adding the potatoes.

Babgulyás
Bean Goulash

Iren Farkas is an occupational therapist, but she and her partner, Janos Levay, the genial local traffic policeman, also raise pigs. As you walk into the courtyard of their house, you're greeted by loud oinking from the closely serried pens.

Most of the pigs are sold, but Iren keeps some of the meat for the family, smoking a good deal of it. She used a strongly flavoured pork tail to add extra 'oomph' to the bean goulash she made us. Though it is not quite the same, my butcher does a good line in smoked pork knuckle, which I used instead. Another ingredient that Iren used is parsley root. Although I've occasionally seen it for sale here, it is a rarity, and knobbly celeriac is the best substitute.

SERVES 8–10 generously

6 pints (3.4 litres) pork or chicken stock or water

1 lb (450 g) dried borlotti beans, soaked overnight and drained

2 onions, quartered

1 medium celeriac, cut into ¾-inch (2-cm) cubes

2 large carrots, sliced ½ inch (1 cm) thick

1 large tomato weighing about 8 oz (225 g), halved

1 medium to large kohlrabi, cut into ¾-inch (2-cm) cubes

1 wax pepper or green pepper, cut in half and seeded

1½ lb (750 g) belly of pork (with rind) cut into 1-inch (2.5-cm) cubes

1 handful of parsley, tied in a bunch

1 small bunch of celery leaves, tied with string

12 oz (350 g) speck or well-smoked bacon, cut roughly into chunks

1 smoked pork knuckle (optional)

5 cloves garlic, peeled but whole

1 tablespoon caraway seeds

5 bay leaves

1½ heaped tablespoons paprika

salt and pepper

To finish

8 oz (225 g) noodles, broken into small pieces

1 large onion, chopped

6 tablespoons dripping or lard

4 tablespoons flour

2 tablespoons paprika

Put the stock or water in an enormous pan and bring to the boil. Add all the ingredients for the main stew, bring back to the boil and simmer, covered, for 2½–3 hours, until the beans and meats are very tender.

About 15 minutes before serving, add the noodles to the *gulyás*. Fry the onion in the dripping or lard until translucent. Sprinkle over the flour and stir for several minutes, until the *roux* cooks to a light biscuit-brown. Draw off the heat and stir in the 2 tablespoons paprika. Gradually mix in 10 fl oz (300 ml) cold water to make a smooth paste, then tip into the soup, stirring constantly. Simmer for a final 5–10 minutes.

Körözött Juhturó
Liptó Cheese Spread

By rights this piquant cheese spread should be made with the Hungarian sheep's milk cheese called Liptó, or at the very least from some other soft sheep's milk cheese. Unfortunately soft young sheep's milk cheese is not that readily available here, so I substitute a fresh goat's milk cheese instead and the result tastes just fine.

Apart from cheese, the ingredients that appear without question in every recipe for this spread I have ever seen are butter, paprika, caraway and onion. Anchovy fillets are sometimes replaced with anchovy paste; capers are entirely optional, though they bring a pleasing touch of sharpness.

Spread on hot toast, this makes a delicious simple first course. It is also very good in sandwiches, spread thickly instead of butter. This recipe makes a fair quantity, but it keeps in the refrigerator for several days so does not have to be eaten at one sitting.

SERVES about 8

8 oz (225 g) fresh goat's milk cheese or curd cheese
4 oz (100 g) butter, softened
3 tinned anchovy fillets, finely chopped
½ small onion, finely chopped
½ teaspoon Dijon mustard
1 teaspoon paprika
½ teaspoon caraway seeds, crushed
½ tablespoon capers, chopped (optional)

Beat the cheese with the butter until smooth. Mix in all the other ingredients. Taste and adjust the flavourings, adding a little more mustard, paprika or whatever until the blend of flavours suits your personal taste. Serve with hot toast.

Paprikás Csirke
Chicken Paprikash

The difference between a paprikás *stew and a* pörkölt *is soured cream, stirred in to enrich the red juices in which the meat cooks. The final sauce should be fairly thick, so if it seems watery, just boil it down for a little longer.*

SERVES 4

1 chicken, cut into 8 pieces
salt and pepper
2 tablespoons lard
1 large onion, grated or finely chopped
1 green pepper, seeded and cut into rings

1 large tomato, weighing about 8 oz (225 g), skinned, seeded and roughly chopped
1 heaped tablespoon paprika
5 fl oz (150 ml) crème fraîche, or soured cream mixed with double cream

Season the chicken with salt. In a heavy casserole melt the lard and add the onion. Stir, then cover and sweat over a low heat for 5 minutes. Add the chicken, green pepper and tomato, cover tightly and cook for a further 10 minutes. Now add the paprika, salt and pepper, stir, then cover again and keep cooking over a very low heat for a further 40 minutes, turning the chicken pieces occasionally and stirring once in a while to prevent catching. When the chicken is cooked and very tender, lift it out of the casserole and reserve.

Skim the fat off the sauce left in the casserole, then boil until reduced by half. Stir in the crème fraîche, bring to the boil, stirring, and simmer for a few minutes until thickened. Taste and adjust the seasoning. Return the chicken to the pan and simmer for a few more minutes to heat through. Serve with *Galuska* (see p.147) or other noodles.

Galuska
Little Egg Dumplings

Tiny irregular dumplings, these Galuska *are served alongside all kinds of stews to sop up the juices, or are added to soups. They are very easy to make, with the added bonus that they don't suffer from being cooked several hours in advance, then re-heated just before serving. They freeze well too.*

SERVES 4

1 egg
1 oz (25 g) lard, melted, then cooled until
　　tepid
5 tablespoons milk or water
salt
8 oz (225 g) plain flour, sifted

To serve

1½ tablespoons lard or butter

Beat the egg lightly with the melted lard, the milk and salt. Mix in the flour to make a soft but firm dough (you may not need quite all of it, but if the dough is sticky add a little extra). Knead briefly to smooth out, then cover with a cloth and rest for 10 minutes.

Bring a large pan of salted water to the boil. Break off tiny knobs of the dough, no bigger than the nail on your little finger, and drop into the water. *Galuska* are meant to be uneven and irregular, so don't try to roll or shape them. After a few minutes skim off those *Galuska* that have bobbed up to the surface, and drain in a colander. Then go back to the dough and carry on. When they are all done, rinse with cold water and drain again.

To serve, melt the remaining lard or butter in a wide pan over a medium heat. Add the *Galuska* and stir until piping hot.

László Marhapörköltje
László's Beef *Pörkölt*

The second cauldron out in the paprika field was filled with beef pörkölt, *a dark, thickly sauced beef stew. The initial slow cooking of the meat with no added water at all is, I think, the key. And when you do add water in the next stage, use as little as possible. The idea is to end up with very tender meat and just enough sauce to coat it, but not to set it swimming.*

SERVES 4–6

2 tablespoons lard
1 large onion, chopped
2½ lb (1.25 kg) stewing beef, cut into
    1-inch (2.5-cm) cubes
1 heaped tablespoon paprika
1 clove garlic, crushed (optional)
1 wax pepper or green pepper, seeded
    and roughly sliced

1 large tomato weighing about 8 oz
    (225 g), skinned and roughly
    chopped
1 hot cherry pepper or dried red chilli
    (optional)
salt and pepper

Melt the lard and add the onion. Cook over a gentle heat until the onion is tender without browning. Add the beef, paprika and garlic (if using). Stir, then half-cover and stew gently in its own juices for about 10 minutes, stirring occasionally. You shouldn't need to add any water, but if by any unforeseen chance it does threaten to burn, add just a tablespoon or two.

Now add the wax or green pepper, tomato and cherry pepper or chilli. Stir, season with salt and pepper, half-cover again and cook for 10 more minutes, again stirring occasionally and adding a little water if absolutely necessary.

Next add just enough water barely to cover the meat. Half-cover with a lid and simmer gently for about 2 hours, until the meat is very tender and the liquid has reduced to a rich, dark, unctuous sauce. Taste and adjust the seasoning, and then serve.

Báránypörkölt Juhász Módra
Shepherd's Lamb *Pörkölt*

While William, Sarolta and Jozsef, the shepherd, went riding across the puszta, *this* pörkölt *of lamb, an expensive treat, was simmering over the fire. The shepherd's wife Ilona added barely enough water to prevent burning, then left the stew to its own devices.*

SERVES 6

2½ lb (1.25 kg) lean lamb, cut into 1-inch (2.5-cm) cubes
2 onions, diced
1½ heaped tablespoons paprika
3 tablespoons tomato purée
1 heaped teaspoon caraway seeds

salt and pepper
1 wax pepper or green pepper, seeded and quartered
1 large tomato, skinned, seeded and roughly chopped
1 hot cherry pepper or dried red chilli

Layer the lamb and onions in a heavy-based casserole. Spoon over the paprika, tomato purée, caraway seeds and a grind or two of black pepper. Pour in about 2 fl oz (50 ml) water. Bring slowly to the boil, then simmer very slowly, uncovered, for about 30 minutes, stirring occasionally. The meat should cook in its own juices, but if it threatens to burn, add a few more spoonfuls of water.

Now add the remaining ingredients (including some salt), and simmer for a further 1 hour–1 hour 20 minutes, stirring occasionally and adding water if needed, until the meat is tender and bathed in a rich dark sauce. Taste and adjust the seasoning.

Töltött Vesepecsenye
Vera's Stuffed Pork Fillet

When Vera buys pork fillet for a Töltött Vesepecsenye, *she just asks her butcher to make a hole through the centre of each piece so that she can stuff it like a sausage. I don't think many butchers here would do that, though if you have a sausage-making attachment for your mixer, it might be worth asking, as it certainly makes life easier.*

Otherwise you'll have to do a nifty bit of knifework, so that you can open the fillet out flat into a rectangle – not half as difficult as it may appear at first.

SERVES 6

2 pork fillets
2 oz (50 g) lard
2 lb (900 g) potatoes, peeled and thickly
    sliced

Stuffing

1 lb (450 g) minced pork
4 cloves garlic, crushed
1 level teaspoon ground black pepper
1½ heaped tablespoons paprika

1 heaped teaspoon ground cumin
2 tablespoons lard
salt

To make the stuffing, mix all the ingredients together, then pass through a mincer or process until smooth.

Now the tricky but by no means impossible bit – making cuts in the fillets so that you can open each one out flat in a rectangle. Using a really sharp knife, make a cut along the length of each fillet, from one end to the other, about a third of the way up its thickness, without cutting right through to the far side. Now make a similar cut along the other side, about a third of the way down from the top, from one end to the other and again without cutting right the way through. If this sounds confusing, think in terms of cutting the meat so that it concertinas neatly. If that doesn't help, look at the diagram opposite.

Open the meat out flat and sandwich each piece between 2 sheets of greaseproof paper. Using a rolling pin, flatten it out to form a fairly large rectangle. Don't get too enthusiastic or you'll end up with holes. Season with salt and pepper.

Divide the stuffing between the two pieces of fillet, making a nice sausage down the length of each one, and flipping over the ends to enclose the filling. Roll it up neatly and tie firmly along its length, or sew it up with a needle and thread.

Preheat the oven to 350°F (180°C), gas mark 4. Grease a roomy roasting tin generously with half the lard and lay the stuffed fillets in it. Snuggle the potato slices around the meat and dot the whole lot with the remaining lard. Spoon over 4 tablespoons water. Cover with foil and bake in the oven for 1 hour, basting occasionally. The potatoes and pork should be fairly well cooked by this time. Uncover, raise the heat to 400°F (200°C), gas mark 6, baste the meat and potatoes with their own juices and return to the oven for a final 10−15 minutes to brown lightly. Serve the fillet sliced, with the potatoes and any pan juices that they haven't sopped up.

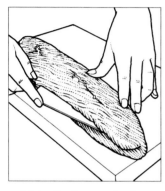

1 Make the first cut in the fillet about ⅓ of the way up its thickness without cutting right through to the far side.

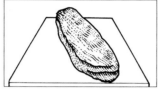

2 Make a similar cut on the opposite side of the fillet.

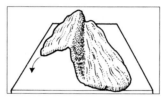

3 Open the meat out flat.

4 Sandwich the fillet between two pieces of greaseproof paper and flatten with a rolling pin to form a fairly large rectangle.

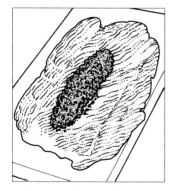

5 Using half the stuffing make a sausage down the length of the flattened pork fillet.

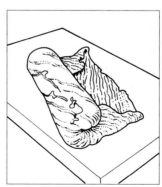

6 Roll up the filling inside the pork fillet, tucking in the sides as you go.

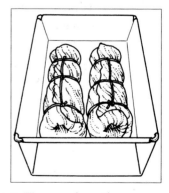

7 Tie up and sew the sausage to keep it in place then lay in a greased roasting tin which will take the second fillet snugly.

Túrós Tészta
Noodles with Curd Cheese

We asked Iren, who cooked the Babgulyás for us, if there was any savoury dish she made that didn't have paprika in it. After a few minutes' thought, she said she could think of only one, and that was Túrós Tészta, though in the normal run of things she might just sprinkle a little paprika over the finished noodles for a hint of colour . . . but not necessarily!

Túró is a lovely, rich, soft cheese which Iren buys from the farmers' market along with soured cream. It tastes a little like Italian ricotta, but is creamier. Túrós Tészta is a mild gentle dish, just right after the heartiness of something like a gulyás.

SERVES 6

1 lb 5 oz (600 g) flat postage-stamp pasta pieces, or lasagne broken into squares roughly the size of a stamp
salt and pepper
6 oz (175 g) speck or smoked streaky bacon, thickly sliced and cut into strips

3 tablespoons lard
1½ lb (750 g) ricotta or curd cheese
5 fl oz (150 ml) crème fraîche, or soured cream mixed with double cream

Preheat the oven to 325°F (160°C), gas mark 3.

Boil the noodles in plenty of salted water until just *al dente*. Drain thoroughly and rinse under the cold tap. Fry the speck in the lard until browned. Strain off the fat and reserve.

Pour a little of the hot fat into a wide shallow baking dish and tip-tilt to cover the base. Spread about one-third of the cooked noodles in the dish. Dot with half the ricotta and half the crème fraîche and season well. Repeat the layers, then cover with the remaining noodles. Scatter over the bacon and drizzle over 4 tablespoons of the reserved fat. Bake in the oven for 25–30 minutes, until lightly browned on top. Serve hot from the oven.

Lecsó
Green Pepper and Tomato Stew

There's no shortage of green peppers and tomatoes throughout the summer months – everyone seems to grow their own, and if they don't the market is piled high with both – and Lecsó is one of the best-known ways of using them up. Though it may well be eaten fresh, a good deal is bottled for the winter months, when it may be used to enliven stews and soups.

It can be served as a vegetable side-dish, or amplified into a meal by the addition of slices of smoked sausage or frankfurters which are poached in the stew. Alternatively, when the Lecsó is cooked, break 4 eggs in it and scramble them quickly – the result is not dissimilar to the French piperade.

SERVES 4

1 onion, halved and sliced
1 oz (25 g) lard
2 rashers smoked streaky bacon, diced
2 teaspoons paprika
1 lb (450 g) wax peppers or green peppers, seeded and sliced

12 oz (350 g) ripe tomatoes, skinned, seeded and roughly chopped
½ tablespoon sugar
salt and pepper

In a large saucepan cook the onion gently in the lard until translucent. Add the bacon, raise the heat slightly and cook until the onion begins to colour. Sprinkle over the paprika, stir, then add all the remaining ingredients. Simmer for about 40 minutes, until very thick. Serve hot.

Ⓥ
Vegyes Téli Savanyúság
Mixed Salad Pickles

A little dish of mixed salad pickles was put before each person at almost every meal we ate in Kalocsa. In hotels and restaurants they are often the only attempt at 'fresh' vegetables, and luckily they are good enough to stand in loco.

Though any number of different vegetables can be used, the main ones should be cabbage (shredded as thinly as is humanly possible) and cucumber, with green peppers ranking second in importance. Carrots are there more for a splash of colour than anything else, so should by no means predominate. Red peppers can be used but will discolour the green of the other vegetables.

ENOUGH to fill a 3-pint (1.75-litre)
preserving jar

about 3½ lb (1.5 kg) mixed vegetables (cucumber, cabbage, green peppers, carrots, etc.)
1 lb (450 g) onions, finely sliced

4 oz (100 g) coarse sea salt
12 oz (350 g) granulated sugar
10 fl oz (300 ml) distilled malt vinegar

Peel and slice the cucumber as thinly as possible. Quarter the cabbage, remove the tough stalk, then shred very finely. Seed the peppers, discard the white inner membranes, then cut into thin strips. Peel or scrape the carrots and slice paper-thin.

Mix the cabbage with the onions and a handful of the salt. Weigh down with a plate and leave for 24 hours in a cool place, turning occasionally. Salt the cucumber, carrots and peppers in the same way, keeping them separate.

Put the sugar and vinegar in a pan and stir over a medium heat until the sugar has completely dissolved. Leave to cool.

Next day drain all the vegetables, rinse and drain again, squeezing them with your hands to expel excess water. Pack them tightly into sterilized jars, building up layers of different vegetables, and tucking discs of carrot in a ring around the outer edge of the central layer, so that they show decoratively through the glass. Pour over the marinade, filling right up to the top. Cover with a clean tea-towel and leave for 24 hours. Top up with marinade if necessary, so that the vegetables are totally covered. Seal tightly with non-corrosive lids and leave in a cool dark place for at least a week before using. The pickles can be stored for up to 3 months or even longer, though the colours will deteriorate.

ⓥ
Mákos Patkó Beigli
Poppy-seed Rolls

I adore the dark nutty poppy-seed fillings of eastern Europe, and was delighted to find a good supply of poppy-seed pastries in a small food shop not far from our hotel. Vera told me that she makes a poppy-seed roll, based on the same yeast dough as she uses for cheesecake, and this is a loose interpretation from her description. If you wish, you can also add raisins or a little grated plain chocolate to the filling. Alternatively you could wrap it in filo pastry to make a type of Strudel *or* rétes *– use the method given for Apple* Strudel *on p.182.*

SERVES 8–10

1 quantity dough as for *Túrós Lepény* (see
    p.158)
1 egg, beaten

Filling

9 oz (250 g) poppy seeds
10 fl oz (300 ml) milk
5 oz (150 g) vanilla sugar, or caster sugar
    plus ½ teaspoon natural vanilla essence

finely grated zest of ½ lemon
1 apple, peeled, cored and coarsely grated

Make the dough and let it rise once. Punch down and knead again for 5 minutes.

While the dough is having its first rising, make the filling. Grind the poppy seeds in an electric spice grinder. Mix the milk with the sugar and bring to the boil. Tip in the ground poppy seeds, stir and bring back to the boil, then draw off the heat. Add the vanilla essence (if using), the lemon zest and grated apple, mix evenly, then leave to cool and thicken, stirring occasionally.

Divide the dough into two. On a lightly floured board, roll each piece into an oval about 13 × 10 inches (33 × 25 cm). Spread half the filling over each one, leaving a clean 1½-inch (4-cm) border all the way round the edges. Brush the borders with beaten egg, then roll up (from the long side, so that the finished rolls are about 13 inches (33 cm) long). Pinch the ends together and tuck underneath. Lay the rolls on floured baking sheets, joins underneath, curving each one into a horseshoe shape. Leave to rise for 30 minutes – 1 hour in a warm place, then chill in the refrigerator for 30 minutes. Prick with a fork, then brush with egg.

Preheat the oven to 425°F (220°C), gas mark 7. Bake the rolls for 10 minutes, then reduce the heat to 350°F (180°C), gas mark 4, and bake for a further 25–30 minutes. Cool on a wire rack.

Ⓥ

Túrós Lepény
Baked Cheesecake

Vera's baked cheesecake proved an enormous hit. She uses an enriched yeast dough as the base, light and fluffy, topped with a blend of soft cheese mixed with soured cream and raisins.

It's important to get the dough stretched out as thinly as possible over the base of the tin, which should, by the way, be more generously greased than usual if you want the dough to be crisp underneath. Inevitably it will rise up unevenly here and there, but that's no disaster.

SERVES 8–10

Dough

7½ fl oz (225 ml) milk	1 lb (450 g) strong plain flour
1 oz (25 g) fresh yeast or ½ oz (15 g) dried yeast	pinch of salt
	4 oz (100 g) butter or duck fat
1 tablespoon caster sugar	1 egg, beaten

Filling

12 oz (350 g) ricotta or curd cheese	3 eggs, separated
7½ fl oz (225 ml) crème fraîche, or double cream mixed with soured cream	3 oz (75 g) caster sugar
	3 oz (75 g) raisins

First make the dough. Warm the milk to blood temperature (it's about right when you can hold your finger in it for 10 seconds only before it feels too hot). Stir in the crumbled yeast and sugar. Leave in a warm place for 5–10 minutes, until frothing.

Sift the flour with the salt. Rub in the butter. Make a well in the centre and add the beaten egg and about two-thirds of the yeast mixture. Mix, gradually drawing in the flour and adding more of the yeast mixture as needed, until you have a soft, slightly sticky dough. Knead vigorously for 10 minutes, until smooth and elastic. Dust with a little flour, cover with a cloth and leave in a warm place until doubled in bulk – about 1–1½ hours.

PREVIOUS PAGES
Left: *Vegyes Téli Savanyúság* (Mixed Salad Pickles) see p.154.
Right: *Vera Szilváslepénye* (Vera's Plum Tart) see p.159.

Punch down, knead again for 5 minutes, then line a thoroughly greased, deep 10 × 14 inch (25 × 35 cm) baking tin with the dough, using your hands to spread it evenly over the base and ease it an inch or so up the sides. Persevere – though it has an infuriating habit of slipping back, you will eventually get it to stretch over the tin. Leave in a warm place for 10 minutes while you make the filling.

Preheat the oven to 350°F (180°C), gas mark 4. To make the filling, beat the ricotta with the crème fraîche until smooth. Add the egg yolks, sugar and raisins and mix. Whisk the egg whites until they form stiff peaks, then fold into the mixture. Spread lightly and evenly over the prepared base. Bake in the oven for about 30–40 minutes, until the filling is just set. Serve warm or cold.

Ⓥ
Vera Szilváslepénye
Vera's Plum Tart

The same yeast dough as used for Túrós Lepény, *but in another entirely different incarnation, this time as the base for a wonderful juicy plum tart. Again, stretch the dough out thinly, then all you need to do is cram as many plum halves as you can on top and dredge it with sugar and cinnamon before baking.*

Use small oval summer plums, in preference to the outsized round ones imported at other times of the year.

SERVES 8–10

1 quantity of dough as for *Túrós Lepény*
2 lb (900 g) small dark plums
4 oz (100 g) caster sugar
1 tablespoon ground cinnamon

Make the dough and line a thoroughly greased baking tin as for *Túrós Lepény*. Halve the plums and remove the stones. Lay the halves on the dough, cut side up, packing them in tightly in a single layer. Mix the sugar and cinnamon and sprinkle over. Leave for 15 minutes in a warm place and meanwhile pre-heat the oven to 350°F (180°C), gas mark 4. Bake the tart in the oven for about 30 minutes. Serve warm or cold, cut into squares.

Ⓥ
Palacsinta
Pancakes

Everyone loves pancakes in Hungary. When Sarolta took me to meet Vera for the first time, we sat down to an afternoon feast of endless pancakes, sweetened with home-made jams, or sugar and cinnamon. Later on we came across pancakes that formed the wrapping for more complicated fillings, such as the savoury Hortobagyi *pancakes or the totally over-the-top Gundel-style sweet pancakes below.*

A good pancake, like the ones Vera makes, is thin and light and never flabby. It may take a few attempts to get it right, but pancake batter is fairly untemperamental and survives a bit of tampering with.

MAKES about 12

6 oz (175 g) flour
pinch of salt
3 eggs
8 fl oz (250 ml) milk

1 teaspoon sugar
8 fl oz (250 ml) fizzy mineral water
clarified butter for cooking (see below)

Sift the flour with the salt and add the sugar. Make a well in the centre and break in the eggs. Add about half the milk. Stir gradually, drawing in the flour and adding the remaining milk slowly, to form a smooth batter. Leave to rest for 30 minutes. Just before using, stir in enough of the mineral water to make a thin batter with the consistency of runny single cream.

Brush a heavy pan, about 8–9 inches (20–23 cm) in diameter, with clarified butter and heat thoroughly. Stir the batter. Pour a small ladleful of batter into the pan, then tip and tilt it so that the batter covers the base. Pour out any excess. As soon as the batter has set and bubbles begin to show on the upper surface, turn the pancake over and cook for a few more seconds until lightly browned underneath. Continue, brushing the pan with butter between pancakes, until all the batter is used up.

The first pancake nearly always sticks, so think of it purely as a tester (and cook's perk). If it is rather thick, thin down the batter with a little extra mineral water. Pile up the pancakes as you cook and keep them warm if you are using them immediately. Serve sweet with jam, or sugar and cinnamon, or sugar and lemon juice.

If you are making the pancakes in advance, or want to freeze them, lay a strip of greaseproof paper between each pair. When cool, wrap neatly in cling film.

To clarify butter

Melt the butter and heat it through, skimming off any scum that rises to the surface. Leave to stand off the heat for a few minutes until the white sediment has settled at the bottom. Carefully pour off the melted butter, leaving the sediment behind.

Ⓥ

Palacsinta Gundel Módra
Gundel-style Pancakes

Well, almost Gundel-style. I've tried the bona-fide *recipe and found the chocolate sauce rather fiddly and complicated, and in the end not so very different from the simpler one I usually make. I also prefer the whipped cream served on the side, rather than folded into the sauce. So, with apologies, I present here my version.*

Karoly Gundel remains Hungary's best-known chef, though he died almost forty years ago. His most famous restaurant, at the city park in Budapest, still retains his name. Palacsinta Gundel Módra, pancakes with a walnut and rum filling, smothered in chocolate sauce, have become part and parcel of the Hungarian culinary repertoire, appearing on menus right across the country.

12 sweet pancakes (see p.160)
1½ oz (40 g) clarified butter (see p.161)
5 fl oz (150 ml) double or whipping
    cream, whipped

Filling

2 oz (50 g) raisins
1 oz (25 g) candied orange peel, chopped,
    or (better, though not quite
    'authentic') the finely grated zest of
    ½ orange
5 tablespoons rum

4 fl oz (120 ml) single cream
8 oz (225 g) coarsely ground walnuts
4 oz (100 g) caster sugar

Chocolate sauce

4 oz (100 g) plain chocolate, grated or
    finely chopped
8 fl oz (250 ml) milk

½ teaspoon natural vanilla essence
4 tablespoons caster sugar
1 oz (25 g) cocoa powder

Make the pancakes in advance, even the day before.

Next tackle the filling. Soak the raisins and candied orange peel or orange zest in the rum for at least 30 minutes, longer if possible. Drain and reserve the rum. Bring the single cream to the boil and stir in the walnuts, sugar, raisins and half the rum. Stir over a low heat for 1 minute, until thickened. Place a large dollop of filling in each pancake and fold in four.

The sauce can be made in advance and re-heated. Put all the ingredients into a pan and stir over a low heat until the sugar and chocolate have completely dissolved. Bring to the boil and simmer for 5 minutes. If necessary, give it a quick whisk or sieve to remove any lumps. Stir in the remaining rum from the raisins.

Shortly before eating, warm up the filled pancakes in the clarified butter over a moderate heat. Re-heat the chocolate sauce and pour over the pancakes. Serve with whipped cream.

Graubünden
SWITZERLAND

Soups and Salads
Bündner Gerstensuppe Barley Soup   p.168
Wurstsalat Sausage Salad   p.178

Main Courses
Härdöpfelpitta Potato and Dried Pear Pancake Squares   p.170
Maluns Fried Potato Crumbs with Apple Compote   p.170
Käsesuppe Bread and Cheese Pudding   p.171
Pizokels (Bizochels) Dumpling Noodles   p.172
Härdöpfel-Pizokels Pizokels with Potatoes and Speck   p.173
Pizokels mit Spinat und Tomaten Pizokels with Spinach and Tomato   p.173
Capuns Chard Parcels   p.174

Desserts
Linzertorte Raspberry and Almond Tart   p.179
Engadiner Nusstorte Caramel Nut Tart   p.180
Flambierte Zwetschgen in Butter überbacken Flambéed Buttered Plums   p.181
Apfelstrudel Apple Strudel   p.182

Breads
Burebrot Farmer's Bread   p.183
Zopf Rich White Bread Plaits   p.184
Birnbrot Dried Pear Bread   p.186

Sundries
Bircher Muesli Fresh Muesli   p.188
Bircher Muesli My Version   p.188

Graubünden
SWITZERLAND

The first thing that struck me about the Swiss countryside was how ridiculously Swiss-looking it was! Pure chocolate-box stuff – wooden chalets and barns, cows with bells on, towering snow-capped mountains, green meadows and huge blue lakes – and this was just what we glimpsed from the train as we chugged towards the Graubünden. That initial impression was never tarnished, though it soon ceased to belong on a chocolate-box, becoming a fully animated, 3-D reality.

I've never in my life wanted to go skiing, I'm not rich enough to need a Swiss bank account, and nor have I yearned for a fondue set. Nothing had ever tempted me to go to Switzerland. Shortly before we set off, I'd been racking my brains, wondering what on earth they did eat there – surely the inhabitants didn't live on chocolate and cheese alone? What intrigues me, now that I'm an out-and-out fan of the country, is why we seem to know so little apart from the obvious clichés.

It was August, high summer, and an idyllic time to be in rural Switzerland, though we began our trip in a town – a small one, Chur, with an old quarter that was as pretty and neat as a picture. On Saturday morning the farmers' market packed out the main pedestrian street, winding its way from the cathedral square. Crowded though it was, the scene was one of orderliness and relaxed bustle, with none of the frenetic pandemonium of a Mediterranean market. At least half, if not more, of the stalls sold organically raised vegetables and produce of impeccable quality: not a limp leaf to be seen. There were superb displays of cheeses and breads, hand-made by small-scale producers. All told, it offered an encouraging promise of meals to come ... though, curiously enough, there was very little chocolate to be seen.

It was the Lerchi family who introduced us properly to local life and food. Freda and Hans Lerchi, their son Conrad and his South African wife Robyn, not to mention their three small children, live in what would be a Heidi house, if it weren't so obviously part of a thriving hard-working farm. To the left of the front door is the old wood-fired bread oven – still used once a week – and facing it, across the lane, a huge two-storey barn for storing hay and for housing the cattle in winter. The Lerchis maintain traditions, not because they know nothing better, nor through

Making cheese in the early morning light.

mere nostalgia. They value, above all, quality of life, and that's something they seem to have in plenty.

Freda has taught Robyn everything she knows about Bündner cooking, or rather the dishes that belong to her native village and the village she lives in now. And that's a considerable amount. The food, as one might well expect in a predominantly dairy farming community in a mountainous area, is hearty and rich – with lots of butter and cheese – and deeply satisfying. After a couple of days' cooking and eating with the Lerchis, we definitely needed a good long hike through the alpine meadows.

This area lies close to the Austrian border, and many dishes overlap – *Linzertorte* and *Strudel* are popular – but we're not that far from Italy either, and there's a distinct Italian flavour to be found. Risotto and polenta are fairly commonplace.

Though the local polenta is made from ground maize, it is quite different from anything I've eaten in Italy. We got our first taste of it high, high up, almost in the clouds, above the village of Brigels. The bi-annual *Alpfest* was being celebrated, beginning with an open-air mass between the two long cow-sheds. Next came the primary school children, shyly and very hesitantly launching into a song-and-dance routine about growing, harvesting, grinding and, naturally, eating polenta. They looked blessedly relieved when their performance ended and it was time for lunch.

Cheese and Stereotypes

Switzerland is unfairly cursed with some uncharitably grim stereotypes. The Swiss, we are led to believe, are thoroughly boring, their trains run on time and, of course, they make famously naff cuckoo clocks. Well, none of this proved to be at all helpful. The first train we took was shockingly late, and dirty, and when we finally arrived in the Graubünden, we had an uproarious time with some of the most fascinating people we met on our travels. Oh yes, and most cuckoo clocks are made in the Black Forest. Travel, you quickly learn, not only broadens the mind, but also teaches you never to rely on stereotypes.

Although it is an immensely wealthy country, Switzerland valiantly refuses to lose its identity, retaining a deliberately small-scale approach to life, especially in politics and agriculture. Subsidizing small farms is seen by the Swiss as an essential element in keeping alive the country's soul, its countryside.

In the dairy we visited, a giant copper bowl sat, perfectly clean and scrubbed, waiting for the morning's milk to be poured gradually in. As the heat from the wood-fired stove below warmed up the whole cauldron, steam drifted upwards and the room filled with a luscious, warm, milky, smell. Together with a little rennet, which causes heated milk to coagulate, this process is the basis of all cheese-making, and how the famous *Alpkäse*, or Alp cheese, has been made for generations. That vital moment when the curds begin to collect comes alarmingly suddenly, and then it's away with all thoughts of quiet and relaxation, for there follows a hectic few minutes of sheer rush.

Both dairymen, looking disturbingly like Rod Stewart in earlier years, stripped to the waist and began pulling a fine muslin net through the steaming liquid to collect the coalescing lumps of curd, lifting it out skilfully with teeth and arms and rushing off towards the cheese moulds laid out on a table. Squeezed and smacked around a bit, the warm curds were pressed in and laid to cool on scrubbed pine planks, before a twenty-four-hour soaking in a brine that had been allowed to 'mature' a little. And this, in essence, is how the cheese is made. Left to mature for about six weeks it continues to ripen with age.

Meanwhile, a water-powered churn turned rhythmically so that while the cheese was being made, the butter slowly began to set. At the end of a hard morning's milking, what better way to breakfast than with a slice of bread, totally fresh butter and a chunk of *Alpkäse*!

Lunch meant great hunks of Brigels cheese and rough country bread, sausages, or overflowing paper plates of *polenta mit rahm* – in other words drenched in an almost obscene flood of thick cream. We sampled it all, crowded on to wooden benches at long trestle tables. The polenta is very coarsely ground, with the texture of proper Scottish oatmeal porridge. It's the kind of thing I love, though William wasn't so keen. Half-way through lunch, the heavens opened and the rain began to pelt down. Everyone grabbed plates, benches, tables – whatever was to hand – and we ended up in the warm sheds, with their amiable smell of cows and milking.

There's a saying that in Switzerland, 'if it isn't illegal, then it's compulsory', and certainly there are laws about surprisingly day-to-day matters, though no one seems to think them unreasonable. The fields and woods hereabout are filled to bursting with edible wild mushrooms, and we couldn't understand why they were left so blatantly unpicked, when locals often talked about their fondness for fungi.

As it turns out, mushroom picking is strictly regulated to certain periods of the month, and only certain days within that period. Each commune has a mushroom controller, who makes sure that no one transgresses, and who helps with identification. In fact there are almost no transgressors, and the result is a superb crop of mushrooms, plenty for all and sundry, undiminished by over-enthusiastic culling.

Tschiertschen, to the east of Chur, takes the crown as the most beautiful village we passed through, and that's saying something. The houses, many of them with painted panels, crowd together, eaves against eaves, with views across the wide Schanfigg valley. This is where Frau Vinzens lives, an elderly lady, who took us up into the fields to find wild herbs. Like many of the old people here, she learnt from her mother and grandmother which plants are edible, what leaves make soothing teas for this or that ailment, which are for flavouring, which to leave well alone.

We came back with a basketful of greenery which she sorted into small bundles: these for drying out in the open air, these for cooking with straight away, these for scenting the sheets and linen. She opened jars of dried flowers, fruit and herbs and made us a reviving tisane, before plying us with her own home-dried apples and pears. Lunch was *pizokels*, somewhere between pasta and dumplings, speckled with finely chopped mountain herbs.

The diet of the Graubünden may be rich in butter and cheese, but it also has a distinctly healthy side to it. Frau Vinzens' appreciation of tisanes and wild herbs is no isolated trait. Grains and cereals form an important part of the diet – Switzerland is the home of muesli – as do huge salads of mixed green leaves, eaten at practically every meal. This health-consciousness is exaggerated to extremes in the famous Swiss sanatoriums and health clinics, but it exists just as surely in ordinary homes.

Bündner Gerstensuppe
Barley Soup

Even in mid-August the weather is distinctly changeable. Most of the time the sun shone from a clear blue sky, but there were a couple of days when the clouds descended, shrouding the valleys in chilly damp mist. On one of these days Robyn made us all Bündner Gerstensuppe *for lunch. It's a meal-in-a-bowl sort of soup, full of bits and pieces, and very welcome when the weather is bad.*

SERVES 6–8 as a main course

2 carrots, diced
½ celeriac root, diced
1 onion, chopped
2 leeks, sliced
2 tablespoons lard
2 tablespoons flour
6 oz (175 g) pearl barley
2 celery leaves, chopped
10 oz (275 g) smoked speck or smoked streaky bacon, thickly sliced and cut into ½-inch (1-cm) strips

4 oz (100 g) air-dried beef or ham (Parma ham can be used), thickly sliced and cut into ½-inch (1-cm) strips
6 oz (175 g) pork rind, cut into wide strips
1 bay leaf
2 sprigs of fresh parsley
salt and pepper
2 large potatoes, diced
¼ cabbage, finely shredded

In a covered pan, sweat the carrots, celeriac, onion and leeks in the lard over a low heat for 10 minutes. Sprinkle over the flour and stir to mix. Add all the remaining ingredients except the potatoes and cabbage. Pour in 3½ pints (2 litres) water, bring to the boil and simmer gently for about 1½–2 hours, until the barley and meats are very tender. Add salt and pepper to taste, then add the cabbage and potatoes and simmer for a further 15–20 minutes, until the potatoes are cooked. Serve with good bread.

Härdöpfelpitta
Potato and Dried Pear Pancake Squares

This is a stunner of a recipe from Freda Lerchi, one that has been made in her family since time immemorial, and which has always gone down particularly well with the children. It may seem odd to mix potatoes with dried pears and bacon, but it's the mixture of contrasting flavours and textures that makes Härdöpfelpitta *so very appealing.*

It's not really a pancake, as it's baked in the oven, but it turns out almost (though not quite) as thin, and the large squares of it can be neatly folded in half to eat with the fingers. In an ideal world Härdöpfelpitta *should be baked in a wood-fired bread oven to get the perfect smoky taste – it was always a treat reserved for baking day – but it cooks pretty well in an ordinary domestic oven.*

SERVES 4

2 lb (900 g) floury potatoes, boiled in their skins

1 oz (25 g) butter, softened

2 fl oz (50 ml) double cream

3 oz (75 g) plain flour, sifted

2½ oz (65 g) dried pears, sliced and soaked for 10 minutes in warm water

salt, pepper and nutmeg

3 oz (75 g) smoked speck or streaky bacon, cut into narrow strips

Preheat the oven to 375°F (190°C), gas mark 5.

Peel the cooked potatoes while they're still hot and pass them through the fine blade of a mouli-legume (or mash very, very thoroughly). Beat in the butter and cream, then sprinkle in the flour. Beat hard to mix thoroughly. Drain the pears well and add those too, and season with salt, pepper and nutmeg.

Grease a 12 × 12 inch (30 × 30 cm) baking tray, and spread the mixture out thinly in it – it should be no more than ½ inch (1 cm) thick at most. Scatter over the pieces of speck or bacon. Bake in the oven for 30–40 minutes, until browned and crisp on top. Cut into large squares and eat hot or warm.

Maluns
Fried Potato Crumbs with Apple Compote

I've never come across anything quite like Maluns *before. Shreds of potato, coated imperceptibly with flour and slowly double-fried, they eventually emerge from the pan with more of a resemblance to fried breadcrumbs than anything else. They are served as a main course, topped with a generous dollop of apple compote.*

It has to be said that making Maluns *is a lengthy process, to be undertaken out of curiosity when you have plenty of time and patience to spare. It is a peasant dish, comfort food for when times were bad and there was precious little in the larder other than a few left-over boiled potatoes and a bag of last autumn's apples. I really like* Maluns, *but even so it's not the kind of thing I shall be cooking too frequently.*

SERVES 4

1 lb (450 g) slightly waxy main-crop
　　potatoes (such as Cara)
5½ oz (150 g) plain flour
salt
2 oz (50 g) lard
1½ oz (40 g) butter

Apple Compote

1 lb (450 g) eating or cooking apples,
　　peeled, cored and roughly chopped
finely grated zest of ½ lemon
sugar to taste

Boil the potatoes *in their skins* for 10 minutes. Drain and cool. Store, covered with a cloth (*not* cling film or foil, which will trap moisture), in the refrigerator for 48 hours.

At some time in the interim make the apple compote. Place the apples and lemon zest in a pan with just enough water to cover the base. Cover and stew over a low heat until the juices begin to run. Raise the heat slightly and stew, still covered, until the apples are very tender. This will take more time if you have used eating apples. Draw off the heat and beat to a purée, adding sugar to taste.

Back to the potatoes. Pull off the skins and grate the potatoes coarsely. Sprinkle over the flour and some salt, then, with your fingers, mix together, rubbing the shreds of potato between your fingers to make sure that each and every piece is coated in flour.

Melt the lard in a wide heavy frying-pan over a low−moderate heat. Add the potato mixture and start stirring and frying gently. Scrape clean the bottom of the pan frequently with a spatula, and tear up the clumps of potato using a fork and the spatula. Keep going; be patient.

Don't let the *Maluns* brown at all or they will harden unpleasantly − lower the heat if necessary. The idea is to dry the mixture out and this takes time − around 30−40 minutes − and constant attendance. Eventually the clumps will get smaller and smaller, and you can abandon the fork, just breaking up the pieces with the spatula. There comes a point when there is barely any need to scrape the bottom of the pan either. This is a sign that you are nearly done for this stage. Carry on for another 5−10 minutes until the potato mixture resembles coarse breadcrumbs − at last! Tip out of the pan onto a plate and wipe the pan clean.

Shortly before serving, melt the butter in the same frying-pan, again over a low−medium heat, and return the *Maluns* to it. Stir and fry gently and constantly as before, for a further 10 minutes or so, until golden-tan but not browned. Taste and season with more salt if needed, then serve with the cold apple compote.

Käsesuppe
Bread and Cheese Pudding

Nothing is wasted in the Lerchi household. Stale bread is saved and used to make Käsesuppe, *a kind of savoury bread pudding − not a soup at all as its name suggests. What follows is a formula rather than a precise recipe, as you never know quite how much bread or cheese will be left over . . .*

butter, softened
slices of slightly stale *Burebrot* (see p.183)
or wholemeal bread, crusts removed

Gruyère cheese, or *Alpkäse*, thickly sliced
salt and pepper
chicken, beef, pork or vegetable stock

Butter a shallow dish. Butter the bread. Cover the base of the dish with slices of bread, buttered side up. Cover with slices of cheese, season with pepper and a little salt and then finish with more slices of bread, buttered side up. Pour over enough stock to come about three-quarters of the way up the bread. Leave to stand for 1 hour.

Preheat the oven to 400°F (200°C), gas mark 6. Bake the pudding in the oven for 20−30 minutes, until the surface is lightly browned and crisp. Serve piping hot.

Ⓥ *Pizokels (Bizochels)*
Dumpling Noodles

Pizokels *or* Bizochels *(and, confusingly, several other spellings as well) are a kind of dumpling, or perhaps a kind of noodle. I can't quite decide which. As with the spelling of their name, there are a fair number of variations on the theme.* Pizokels *may be made with all white flour or a blend of flours or with grated potato in them, or speckled with spinach or onion, or even with wild herbs from the fields, as are those of Frau Vinzens in Tschiertschen.*

Don't be put off by all these variables. Pizokels, *however they come, are terrifically good. I happen to favour those made with a blend of flours – plain mixed with rye or buckwheat for flavour. The dough, or rather batter, is easy to make and doesn't take long to cook. Serve the cooked* Pizokels *plainly, but amply slathered in melted butter with lots of grated cheese, or in one of the two ways that follow. Cooked* Pizokels *can be frozen, and re-heated later in boiling water.*

SERVES 4

5 oz (150 g) plain flour
2 oz (50 g) rye flour or buckwheat flour
1 egg, lightly beaten
½ tablespoon sunflower oil

Sift the flours together and make a well in the middle. Add the egg, oil and 3 fl oz (85 ml) water. Stir, gradually drawing in the flour and adding more water until you have a batter of thick dropping consistency. Beat hard to get rid of any lumps. Let the batter rest for 30 minutes.

Bring a large pan of salted water to a rolling boil. Now for the trickiest bit: tilt the bowl of batter over the pan and, with a knife, slice off ribbons of batter, about 1 inch (2.5 cm) long and ½ inch (1 cm) thick, into the boiling water. Do this in several batches so that the pan never becomes overcrowded. Lift the *Pizokels* out with a slotted spoon when they float back up to the surface. Taste one to make sure that they are cooked through. Serve hot, with sizzling melted butter and cheese or, better still, in one of the following ways.

Härdöpfel-Pizokels
Pizokels with Potatoes and Speck

This is perfect winter food, the kind of thing you really look forward to after a long, cold, beastly day. It's comfort food, filling and satisfying. Mind you, I had no trouble downing a large plateful in the middle of summer, but it did leave me feeling sluggish that afternoon.

SERVES 4 hungry people

1 lb (450 g) main-crop potatoes, cut into 1-inch (2.5-cm) dice	2 oz (50 g) butter
salt and pepper	1 onion, sliced
4 oz (100 g) piece of smoked speck or smoked streaky bacon	1 quantity of *Pizokels* (see p.172)
	3 oz (75 g) Gruyère cheese, grated
	2 tablespoons chopped fresh chives

Cook the potatoes in boiling salted water until just tender. Drain. Dice the speck into ½-inch (1-cm) cubes. Melt half the butter in a frying-pan and fry the speck over a brisk heat until browned. Lift out with a slotted spoon. Add the onion to the pan and fry until browned. Return the speck to the pan along with the *Pizokels*, potato, pepper, salt if needed and the remaining butter. Stir until piping hot, then scoop into a serving dish and scatter over the cheese and chives. Serve immediately.

Ⓥ

Pizokels mit Spinat und Tomaten
Pizokels with Spinach and Tomato

Another variation on Pizokels *with more of an Italian feel to it. Here they are dished up with lots of fresh spinach (substitute frozen if you must, but it isn't the same) and a buttery tomato sauce. Well, this is Switzerland, and butter reigns supreme. Olive oil doesn't get a look in.*

1½ lb (750 g) fresh spinach
3 oz (75 g) butter
12 oz (350 g) tomatoes, peeled, seeded
    and chopped
1 tablespoon tomato purée
½ teaspoon sugar

salt and pepper
1 quantity of *Pizokels* (see p.172)
1 oz (25 g) Gruyère cheese, grated
1 oz (25 g) Parmesan cheese, freshly
    grated, to serve

Trim the tough stalks off the spinach. Wash the leaves thoroughly in several changes of water, shake off the excess moisture but don't dry, then pack into a large pan. Cover tightly and place over a medium heat. After a few minutes, check to make sure that the juices are beginning to run. Raise the heat, keep covered and cook for a few minutes, stirring once or twice, until the leaves have all collapsed. Drain thoroughly.

In a large wide pan, melt 2 oz (50 g) of the butter. Add the tomatoes, tomato purée, sugar, salt and pepper and cook over a brisk heat until the tomatoes begin to collapse, squishing them down with the back of a spoon. Once you have a rough buttery sauce, add the *Pizokels*, spinach and remaining butter to the pan. Stir for a few minutes, until piping hot. Taste and adjust the seasoning, then turn into a warm serving bowl and sprinkle with Gruyère. Serve immediately, passing around the Parmesan for those who want it.

Capuns
Chard Parcels

Capuns *are made from much the same doughy batter as* Pizokels, *but it is flavoured with herbs and salty air-dried ham and speck. Each nugget of the dough is swaddled neatly in a chard leaf, ending up with a remarkable resemblance to Greek and Turkish stuffed vine leaves.*

When Freda Lerchi makes Capuns, *she uses a multigrain flour that is widely sold in Switzerland, but not available here. Instead I'd suggest adding buckwheat or rye flour to improve the flavour. She usually makes far more than the family can eat at one sitting, freezing the rest, once they are poached, for another meal. The Lerchis always serve* Capuns *with a milky gravy, but I've got to admit a sneaking preference for butter and cheese.*

SERVES 8

10 oz (275 g) plain flour
4 oz (100 g) rye flour or buckwheat flour
2 eggs, lightly beaten
1 tablespoon sunflower oil
4 oz (100 g) air-dried ham, thickly sliced
4 oz (100 g) smoked speck or smoked
    streaky bacon, thickly sliced

1½ tablespoons chopped fresh parsley
½ tablespoon chopped celery leaves
½ tablespoon chopped fresh mint
pepper
about 2½ lb (1.25 kg) chard or spinach
    leaves
2 pints (1.2 litres) ham or beef stock

To finish

10 fl oz (300 ml) creamy milk or single
    cream, or 3 oz (75 g) butter, 2 oz
    (50 g) freshly grated Parmesan cheese
    and 3 oz (75 g) grated Gruyère
    cheese

Sift the flours together and make a well in the middle. Add the eggs, oil and 5 fl oz (150 ml) water. Stir, gradually drawing in the flour and adding more water until you have a batter of thick dropping consistency. Beat hard to get rid of any lumps.

Dice the ham and speck and beat into the flour mixture with the herbs and some pepper. The ham and bacon should provide enough salt.

Cut out the thick stems from the chard (or snip off the stems of spinach), then drop into a pan of boiling water. Bring back to the boil and drain. Dry the blanched leaves on kitchen paper.

Now you must use common sense. If the leaves are large, cut them into quarters, snipping out the central rib. Smaller leaves may be better cut into three or halved. The ideal size for each piece of leaf is about 4 inches (10 cm) wide at the base and about 4 inches (10 cm) long, probably tapering to a point, but of course few of the leaves are going to be snippable into the ideal. Bear in mind that it doesn't matter if there is the odd tear here or there, or if each little parcel of leaf and filling is not perfectly identical . . . far from it.

Place a generous teaspoon of the batter on the widest end of each piece of leaf and flip over the sides, then roll up to form a little parcel about the size of a cork. Don't worry if a spot of filling threatens to ooze out here or there – it'll set quickly as it cooks.

To cook, pour a 1½-inch (4-cm) depth of stock into a wide pan. Bring to the boil and add enough of the leaf parcels to fill the pan in a single layer. Poach for 10–15 minutes, until firm and cooked through (bite into one to check). Lift out with a slotted spoon and arrange in a warm dish. Cover and keep warm while you cook the remaining *Capuns*.

To serve, add the milk or cream to the stock, then boil down until reduced to about 10 fl oz (300 ml) of milky gravy, season and pour over the *Capuns*. Alternatively dot the *Capuns* generously with the butter, scatter over the freshly grated Parmesan and Gruyère, and bake in the oven, pre-heated to 400°F (200°C), gas mark 6, for 15 minutes, until lightly browned and sizzling hot.

Wurstsalat
Sausage Salad

There's a sausage salad on the menu of every inn, and we developed a great liking for the mixture of thinly sliced sausage, cheese and gherkins, dressed with a runny cross between mayonnaise and a vinaigrette. Sometimes Wurstsalat *comes* garniert – *amplified with heaps of shredded carrot, beetroot, cucumber, wedges of tomato and other small salads, all around the edge of the plate.*

SERVES 4 as a starter
or 2 hungry people as a main course

½ onion, sliced
4 oz (100 g) cabbage, finely shredded
salt
4 saveloys or cervelas weighing about 8 oz
    (225 g) in total

4 oz (100 g) Gruyère or Emmenthal
    cheese, sliced
3 large gherkins, finely chopped
2 tablespoons chopped fresh chives
4–6 lettuce leaves, depending on size

Dressing

1½ tablespoons white wine vinegar
1 tablespoon Dijon mustard
1½ tablespoons mayonnaise
salt and pepper
6 tablespoons sunflower or olive oil

Mix the onion with the cabbage in a bowl. Sprinkle with salt, turn to coat thoroughly and leave for 1 hour, turning occasionally. Rinse and drain well, squeezing with your hands to expel the excess moisture.

Make the dressing by stirring together the vinegar, mustard, mayonnaise, salt and pepper, then gradually beating in the oil. Taste and adjust the seasoning.

Skin and cut the sausage into slices about ⅛ inch (3 mm) thick, then cut each slice in half if small or into ¼-inch (5-mm)-wide strips if of larger girth. Cut the sliced cheese into ¼-inch (5-mm)-wide strips about 1½ inches (4 cm) long. Mix with the sausage, cabbage and onions, gherkins and chives. Just before serving, toss with enough of the dressing to coat nicely. Arrange the lettuce leaves on one large plate and pile the *Wurstsalat* on top.

PREVIOUS PAGES
Background: *Capuns* (Chard Parcels) see p.174.
Foreground: *Linzertorte* (Raspberry and Almond Tart) see p.179.

(V)

Linzertorte
Raspberry and Almond Tart

Like the Engadiner Nusstorte, Linzertorte *has travelled to Chur (from across the Austrian border) and made a second home there. I bought a particularly good individual* Linzertorte *from a farmer's wife at the Saturday market, fully intending to take only a small nibble for purely professional purposes, but of course I ended up eating the whole thing.*

In essence it is a glorified form of almond shortbread, rolled out thickly to line a tart tin. A thin layer of raspberry jam covers it, topped with a lattice of pastry. The quality of the jam will regulate the quality of the final tart. Home-made is best, but otherwise a really good bought one, made with a high proportion of fruit to sugar, is essential.

Since the dough is very rich, it can be a little tricky to handle. Don't worry. Press the dough into the tin, and use your fingers to smooth over any tears or holes. Lay the dough strips over the jam using a palette knife. If the odd one breaks as you lay it down, just pinch the ends together: as the whole tart is dusted with icing sugar before serving, it won't show too much.

SERVES 6–8

5 oz (150 g) flour	finely grated zest of 1 lemon
½ teaspoon ground cinnamon	5 oz (150 g) butter, softened
pinch of salt	2 egg yolks
5 oz (150 g) caster sugar	7 oz (200 g) best-quality raspberry jam
5 oz (150 g) ground almonds	icing sugar

Sift the flour with the cinnamon and salt. Mix with the sugar, ground almonds and lemon zest. Make a well in the centre and place the butter and egg yolks in it. Using a palette knife at first, and then the tips of your fingers, work to a dough. Knead briefly to smooth out. Break off about a quarter of the pastry and wrap in cling film. Wrap the larger part in cling film, then chill both for 30 minutes.

Roll out the larger ball of pastry (leave the rest in the refrigerator for the moment) to a thickness of ¼ inch (5 mm) and line a 9½-inch (24-cm) buttered and floured tart tin with it. Prick with a fork and spread evenly with the jam. Roll out the remaining pastry and trimmings and cut into long strips ½ inch (1 cm) wide. Use these to make a lattice pattern over the jam, pressing the ends on to the edge of the pastry case. Rest for 30 minutes in the refrigerator.

Place a baking tray in the oven, and pre-heat to 400°F (200°C), gas mark 6. Set the tart on the hot baking tray and cook for 25–30 minutes, until nicely browned. Cool and dust lightly with icing sugar before serving.

Ⓥ
Engadiner Nusstorte
Caramel Nut Tart

The Engadiner valley is a fair drive from Chur, but not too far for its famous Nusstorte, *with its rich, caramelized nut filling, enclosed in a double layer of biscuity pastry, to have made the journey. Pastry shops, and indeed stall-holders on the market, have plenty to sell to the passer-by, and it's definitely not to be missed. However, if you're not heading in that direction, here's the recipe.*

SERVES 6–8

11 oz (300 g) plain flour
pinch of salt
7 oz (200 g) butter, chilled and diced
4 oz (100 g) sugar
1 egg plus 1 egg yolk

Filling

11 oz (300 g) sugar
10 fl oz (300 ml) double cream
8 oz (225 g) walnuts, chopped
4 oz (100 g) hazelnuts, chopped
4 oz (100 g) almonds, chopped

To glaze

1 egg yolk mixed with 1 tablespoon milk

To make the pastry, sift the flour with the salt and rub in the butter. Stir in the sugar. Beat the egg and yolk together and add to flour. Mix to form a soft dough. Rest the pastry in the refrigerator for 30 minutes. Roll out just over half of it, and line a 9–10-inch (23–25-cm) straight-sided tart tin.

To make the filling, put the sugar into a pan with 4 tablespoons water. Stir over a moderate heat, without letting it boil, until the sugar has completely dissolved. Brush down any crystals stuck to the side of the pan with a brush dipped in cold water. Stop stirring. Bring to the boil and boil hard for 5–10 minutes, until it caramelizes to a rich brown.

Draw off the heat and pour in the cream at arm's length (it will spit). Swirl it around to dissolve the caramel, then return to the heat. Stir in the nuts and bring back to the boil. Cool for a few minutes until warm rather than hot, then spread in the pastry case.

Roll out the remaining pastry to form a lid. Brush the edges of the case with a little of the egg glaze, then cover with the lid, pressing it gently into place inside the tin. Rest for 30 minutes in the refrigerator.

Brush the pastry with egg glaze. Place in a cold oven and set to 425°F (220°C), gas mark 7. After 15 minutes reduce the heat to 350°F (180°C), gas mark 4, and bake for a further 20 minutes, until lightly browned.

ⓥ
Flambierte Zwetschgen in Butter überbacken
Flambéed Buttered Plums

This is a lovely pudding, quick to make, mildly boozy and with a hint of drama. Serve with vanilla ice-cream, or just plain single cream.

SERVES 4

1 lb (450 g) quetsch or other dark plums
   (Victorias work well)
2 oz (50 g) butter
3 oz (75 g) sugar
1½ fl oz (40 ml) brandy

Split the plums in half and discard the stones. Melt the butter in a wide frying-pan and add the plum halves in a single layer, cut side up. Sprinkle over the sugar. Cover with a large plate or foil and cook over a low heat for 5 minutes. Turn the plums over, shake the pan gently to help the sugar dissolve, then cover again and cook for a further 5 minutes, still over a low heat. Warm the brandy gently in a small pan without letting it boil.

To serve, either divide the plums and their syrup between 4 shallow plates, or place them in a warmed shallow serving dish. Set light to the warm brandy and pour, flaming gaily, over the plums. Take carefully to the table before the flames die down.

Ⓥ

Apfelstrudel
Apple Strudel

Though I'm sure many Swiss cooks would protest that Strudel and filo dough are not quite the same thing, I've found that filo pastry makes a very good wrapping for a Strudel. Lucky, as it happens, since I've never had much success when I've tried my hand at making Strudel pastry, always ending up with more holes than anything else.

As with all pastry dishes, a Strudel is best when it has only recently emerged from the oven, before it has a chance to get soggy and flabby. The breadcrumbs or semolina absorb some moisture from the filling, retarding the process, but they can't stop it altogether.

SERVES 6–8

6 sheets filo pastry, each about 19 × 12 inches (47.5 × 30 cm)	2 tablespoons dry breadcrumbs or semolina
2 oz (50 g) butter, melted and cooled until tepid	icing sugar

Filling

1½ lbs (750 g) eating apples, peeled, cored and diced small	3½ oz (90 g) caster sugar
finely grated zest and juice of ½ lemon	1 heaped teaspoon ground cinnamon
	1½ oz (40 g) raisins

Mix all the filling ingredients together. Pre-heat the oven to 375°F (190°C), gas mark 5.

To prevent the filo pastry drying out, lay it in a heap, cover with a sheet of greaseproof paper and cover that with a tea-towel wrung out in cold water. Lay a large (dry) sheet of greaseproof paper on the work surface. Take 1 sheet of filo pastry and lay it out flat in front of you on the greaseproof paper. Brush with melted butter. Take the next sheet and lay it out flat, overlapping the first along the edge by about 3 inches (7.5 cm). Brush with butter. The third sheet is laid exactly over the first, then brushed with butter, the fourth over the second, then brushed with butter, and so on until all the pastry is used up.

Sprinkle the dry breadcrumbs or semolina over the top two-thirds of the filo pastry, leaving a 1½-inch (4-cm) border. Dollop the apple mixture over the semolina and smooth down lightly to cover. Flip the 1½ inches (4 cm) of bare edge over the filling. Now, starting at the top, roll up the pastry round the apple filling, using the greaseproof paper to help you. Carefully lift on to a greased baking tray and curve round into a horseshoe shape. Brush the top with any remaining butter.

Bake in the oven for 30–40 minutes, until lightly browned and crisp. Poke a skewer into the centre of the *Strudel* to see if the apple is tender. Loosen the *Strudel* with a knife, then slide carefully on to a serving dish, dust with icing sugar and serve hot with cream.

Ⓥ

Burebrot
Farmer's Bread

Burebrot *is the common daily bread of the mountains, with a crisp crust and firm, slightly chewy interior. Freda makes it in big batches – around twenty-four 1 kg loaves at a time – judging the ingredients by eye and mixing the dough in a wooden kneading trough, bleached white by years of scrubbing. While it rises, Hans stokes up the wood-fired oven beside the house. This old-fashioned bread-oven gives the bread a marvellous flavour and a crisp, chewy crust. Some of the bread is sold to local restaurants, the rest kept for the family.*

Freda uses a mixture of flours, including a multigrain one that is not, to my knowledge, available here, more's the pity. The trio of white, wholemeal and rye flour is only an approximation, but it's not a bad one.

MAKES 1 large loaf

1 oz (25 g) fresh yeast or ½ oz (15 g) dried yeast
1 level teaspoon caster sugar
12 oz (350 g) strong white bread flour
10 oz (275 g) wholemeal flour
6 oz (175 g) rye flour
1 tablespoon salt

Crumble the yeast into 10 fl oz (300 ml) warm water and add the sugar. Stir and leave in a warm place for 5–10 minutes, until foaming. Mix the flours and salt and make a well in the centre. Pour in the yeast liquid and mix, gradually adding enough warm water to form a soft but not sticky dough. Knead vigorously for 10 minutes, until smooth and elastic. Return to the bowl, sprinkle with a little extra flour and cover with a cloth. Leave at room temperature for 2–3 hours, until doubled in bulk.

Punch down and knead again for 5 minutes. Shape into a large round loaf and place on a greased baking tray. Leave to rise again, dusted with flour and covered with a cloth, for a further 30 minutes or so.

Preheat the oven to 425°F (220°C), gas mark 7. Make criss-cross slashes across the surface of the dough, then bake for 35–45 minutes, until cooked. Test by tapping the underneath – if it sounds hollow, the loaf is done. Cool on a wire rack.

Ⓥ
Zopf
Rich White Bread Plaits

While Freda makes the Burebrot, Robyn has become the household expert in Zopf production. Zopf means 'plait', but it is always a plait of enriched white-flour dough – Sunday bread for high days and holidays. The first time I watched her deftly plaiting the sausages of dough, I was totally bemused. I couldn't for the life of me work out the pattern, though I was sure there must be one. Second time around she took it slowly, explaining the principle as she went along, and, thank heavens, it made sense, not to mention a pleasingly plump plait. If you follow the diagrams you'll soon get the hang of it.

MAKES 2 plaits

2¼ lb (1 kg) strong white bread flour
1 tablespoon salt
5 oz (150 g) butter
1 generous pint (600 ml) milk
1 teaspoon caster sugar

1 oz (25 g) fresh yeast, crumbled, or ½ oz (15 g) dried yeast
2 eggs
1 egg yolk, mixed with 1 tablespoon water, to glaze

Sift the flour with the salt. Put the butter into a pan with the milk and sugar and warm over a gentle heat, stirring occasionally, until the butter has melted, without allowing it to boil. If necessary, let the mixture cool until it reaches blood temperature. To test roughly, try sticking your finger into the liquid. If you can hold it there for a slow count of 10, but no longer, the heat is about right. Stir in the yeast and leave for 5–10 minutes in a warm place, until foaming.

Gradually stir the eggs and the yeasted milk mixture into the flour to give a soft but not sticky dough. You may not need quite all of the liquid. Knead for 10 minutes, then return to the bowl, sprinkle the surface with a little extra flour, cover with a cloth and leave in a warm place to rise for about 1½–2 hours until double its original bulk.

Punch the dough down and knead for 5 minutes. Divide into 2 pieces. Take the first piece and divide in half. Roll each bit out to make a long sausage, slightly thicker in the centre than at the ends. Plait as shown in the diagram below. Gather the ends together and tuck underneath, then lay on a floured baking tray. Repeat with the remaining dough. Leave the plaits to rise again in a warm place, until almost doubled in bulk – about 1 hour. Now chill in the refrigerator for 30 minutes.

Preheat the oven to 400°F (200°C), gas mark 6. Brush the plaits with the egg glaze, then bake in the oven for 30 minutes. Tap them underneath – if they sound hollow, they're done. Cool on a wire rack.

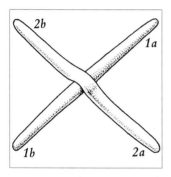

FOLD 1 Lay the two strips of dough in a cross as above.

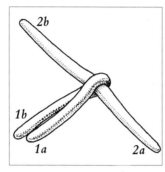

FOLD 2 Fold end 1a to bring it parallel to end 1b placing it over the top strip (2b–2a).

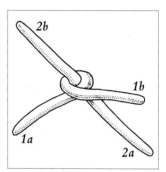

FOLD 3 Fold end 1b over the top strip (2b–2a) and take it up to the top right hand part of the cross where 1a was originally positioned.

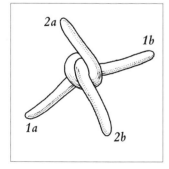

FOLD 4 Swap the position of end 2a and 2b, moving 2a first.

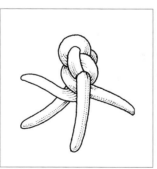

FOLD 5 Continue to cross the ends over in the sequence and direction given in folds 2–4.

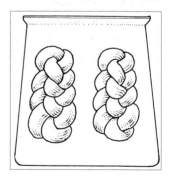

Tuck under the loose ends and leave to rise in a warm place.

Ⓥ

Birnbrot
Dried Pear Bread

Though Birnbrot *is sold throughout the year, it is really a Christmas treat. It's not a bread proper, but nor is it quite a cake. The thin outer casing of yeast dough is wrapped around a moist juicy mush of dried pears and other dried fruit and nuts, solid enough to be sliced, but not too dense to enjoy.*

There are several versions of Birnbrot *(in one the fruit is mixed with the dough), but this recipe, the result of some experimentation, comes close to the one William and I liked best when we were in Switzerland. It might be worth pointing out that* Birnbrot *is something that grows on you. We both thought it quite nice at first, but soon became decidedly enthusiastic.*

MAKES 2 loaves

½ quantity *Zopf* dough (see p.184)
1 egg yolk, mixed with 1 tablespoon
water, to glaze

Filling

12 oz (350 g) dried pears, chopped
4 oz (100 g) prunes, pitted and chopped
2 oz (50 g) raisins
2 oz (50 g) sultanas
1½ oz (40 g) candied peel, chopped
finely grated zest of ½ lemon
3 tablespoons brandy or kirsch
10 fl oz (300 ml) red wine

generous pinch of ground cloves
¼ teaspoon each ground nutmeg,
    coriander, cinnamon and aniseed
1 oz (25 g) blanched almonds, finely
    chopped
1 oz (25 g) pine nuts
3 oz (75 g) walnuts, finely chopped

For the filling, soak all the dried fruit with the lemon zest, brandy and wine overnight. Spoon into a saucepan, adding enough water to come about two-thirds of the way up the fruit. Bring to the boil and simmer, stirring occasionally, until virtually all the liquid has evaporated, leaving a moist mush of fruit. Mash roughly and stir in the remaining filling ingredients. Leave to cool.

Make the *Zopf* dough in advance and leave to rise once. Punch down and knead again for 5 minutes. Divide the dough in half. Take the first half and roll out to form a rectangle about 10 × 12 inches (25 × 30 cm). If necessary, turn it so that one of the long sides is nearest to you. Spread half the fruit mixture thickly over the dough, leaving a 1½–2-inch (4–5-cm) border all the way round. Brush the edges with egg glaze. Roll up tightly to form a tubby sausage. Pinch the narrow ends together and tuck away underneath the roll. Lift on to a floured baking tray with the joins neatly tucked underneath and out of sight. Repeat with the remaining dough and filling.

Prick the upper surface of both rolls, then leave in the refrigerator for 1 hour. Pre-heat the oven to 350°F (180°C), gas mark 4. Brush the rolls with egg glaze and bake in the oven for 30–35 minutes, until browned. Cool on a wire rack. Serve warm or cold, thickly sliced. Once cool, the *Birnbrot* can be wrapped in cling film and kept for up to 1 month.

Ⓥ

Bircher Muesli
Fresh Muesli

Dr Bircher-Benner ran his own exclusive sanatorium, which still exists in the hills overlooking Zurich. Diet was of fundamental importance to his health cures, and each day began with a bowl of his special muesli. His original recipe contained only oats, condensed milk, lemon juice, nuts, apple and other fresh fruit.

SERVES 2

2 heaped tablespoons rolled oats
2 tablespoons condensed milk
juice of ½ lemon
1 apple, grated

2 tablespoons chopped nuts (almonds, walnuts, hazelnuts, etc).
fresh fruit (1 peach, strawberries, blackberries, etc.)

Soak the oats in 3 tablespoons water for at least 20 minutes. Mix in the condensed milk, lemon juice, grated apple and nuts. Divide between 2 bowls and top with fresh fruit, cut up if large.

Ⓥ

Bircher Muesli: My Version

This how I make Bircher muesli, a treat we often have on Sunday mornings. It is not so very different from the original. I've merely replaced the condensed milk and lemon juice with thick yoghurt and honey. I don't usually add nuts, but the grated apple is essential for both texture and flavour.

SERVES 2

2 heaped tablespoons rolled oats
3 tablespoons milk or water
2 – 3 tablespoons Greek-style yoghurt or fromage frais
1 – 2 tablespoons honey

1 apple, grated
fresh fruit (1 peach or 1 banana, blackberries, strawberries or raspberries, etc.)

Soak the oats in the milk or water for at least 20 minutes. Mix in the yoghurt, honey and grated apple. Divide between 2 bowls and top with fresh fruit, cut up if large.

Lofoten Islands
NORWAY

Soups and Starters

Neslesuppe Nettle Soup   p.194
Henningsvaer Fiskesuppe Henningsvaer Fish Soup   p.195
Gravlaks Cured Salmon with Mustard and Dill Sauce   p.196
Torskekaviar Fresh Cod Caviar   p.198

Main Courses

Pytt i Panne Meat and Potato Hash   p.199
Fiskepudding, Fiskeboller eller Fiskekaker Fish Pudding, Fish Balls or
        Fish Cakes   p.202
Fiskegrateng Fish Gratin   p.205
Skrei Kokt med Leversaus Boiled Cod with Liver Sauce   p.206

Sauces

Rekesaus Shrimp Sauce   p.204
Egg- og Smøsaus Egg and Butter Sauce   p.207
Gulrotstuing Carrot Stew   p.207

Desserts

Rømmegrøt Sour-cream Porridge   p.208
Brødpudding med Epler Bread Pudding with Apples   p.209

Lofoten Islands
NORWAY

W̶e stepped off the plane as the light was beginning to fade, straight into a fairy-tale landscape. Around us all was white and pure, from the high peaks of the mountains down to the silver blue of the fjord, glimmering in the last of the sunlight. The airport, little more than a roomy hut, was the only building to be seen. In the twilight the first few flakes of snow began to fall, and I, one who loathes cold weather as a rule, was instantly and utterly smitten.

We shared what seemed to be the only taxi with two genial flooring salesmen from Oslo, into Svolvaer, the main town of the Lofoten Islands. And then we turned our backs on this smudge of civilization to travel on, along seemingly perilous, ice-packed roads (only one heart-stopping skid that night), through the tunnels and bridges that link one island to the next, until at last we found our way to the fishing hamlet of Mortsund.

Mortsund is fairly typical of the small fishing communities in the Lofoten, with a single family running the show, in this case the Statles, our hosts. It is they who run the local shop and restaurant, not to mention the snug *rorbuer* that are let out to tourists.

A *rorbu*, for the uninitiated, is a little wooden house, once the seasonal home of the fishermen who sailed to these islands during the winter months to work the seas that teemed with cod. *Rorbuer* are built clustered together on the water's edge, or even on stilts jutting right out over the lapping waves. We woke in the morning to the gentle plash of the sea and a spectacular view.

Inevitably fish is what it's all about here, and from January through to April most of that fish is cod. I've never seen so much in my life, and never eaten more in one short week. Every morning the boats unload their generous haul of cod, not only in Mortsund but in every inlet and harbour around the island. With practised speedy motions, the fishermen's sharp knives lop off the heads and clean out the innards, separating the precious liver from the discards.

Usually there's a young boy somewhere around – in Mortsund the youngest of the three Statle boys – who grabs the heads, spikes them one by one, to cut out the tongues. It's a pocket-money job, but a highly coveted one.

Cod is Great

The Lofoten Islands, tucked well into the Arctic Circle, stretch somewhat hopefully southwards, towards the warmth of the world. They are far from it. Living almost entirely from the ocean, the Lofot people have benefited from the warm Gulf Stream that keeps the seas up here largely free of ice, but the climate is, to say the least, a little on the harsh side. A second blessing is the abundance of fish, comparative abundance admittedly, for here, as almost everywhere else in the world, fish stocks are in great danger from overfishing. During winter the islands are buzzing with activity, for the waters off the Lofoten are the spawning grounds of cod known as *skrei* and this is the time they arrive, swimming down from the Barents Sea towards the southern end of the islands.

You will see, scattered along the coast, hundreds of wooden racks that – in summer at least – seem rather forlorn. In winter freshly caught cod are tied in pairs and suspended in endless rows along the racks, adding a strange and colourful sight to the snow-whitened hills behind. The air is cold, very cold, and will quickly dry the hanging fish that in time becomes stockfish, or wind-dried cod. Although the process is an ancient one, it is a risky business. A sudden thaw could be disastrous, so a careful eye has to be kept on the weather before the cod are hung out to dry. A somewhat safer way to preserve cod is through salting. This has become a key industry for both Norway and the Lofoten Islands, the resulting *klippfisk* having been traded for generations with the fish-hungry south of Europe. The marvellous thing about cod is that it is a shoaling fish and can arrive in vast numbers. Before the days of refrigeration these ancient methods of preservation proved invaluable, and were the only way to deal with the huge quantities of fish landed.

It was the same dried cod which provided the Lofot and the Vikings with a vital resource that nourished them on their travels. Today, most Lofoten dried cod is sold to Italy (stoccafisso) in response to the Christian need for large quantities of fish for Lent and fast days, which the Mediterranean basin could not satisfy.

In a strange little twist to the story, the word 'stockfish' is not actually derived from either Norwegian or Italian, but Dutch – more precisely from the word *stocvisch*, meaning a fish dried to a *stoc* or stick. When the Dutch began to take over the role of trading intermediary between Northern and Southern Europe in the seventeenth century the Dutch word seems to have become accepted in English. It's one of the very few that have.

The tongues of the fish are considered a great delicacy, eaten fried or boiled, and indeed they are very good, as we soon discovered. They're not the only odd scrap to be savoured. The livers – those that don't go to the cod liver oil stills – are eaten fresh, made into a sauce that is, unexpectedly, as delicious as cod liver oil is vile. This is just the beginning. We were taken to a special cod dinner where every conceivable part of the beast was dished up – tongues and liver, naturally, but also stomach, lips, the juicy little bit from the top of the head, and God alone knows what else. There's even an enterprising jewellery maker on the islands who is transforming the inedible bones into earrings ... and I've a very fetching pair to prove it.

Wenche Lesniak has worked so long with the Statles that she has become part of the family. She knows every itinerant fisherman and, it seems, practically everyone else on the whole string of islands. Wenche and Åse Statle are also marvellous cooks, in the traditional style. The cooking here is simple, based inevitably on an abundance of fish, and a limited selection of other high-quality ingredients, particularly the devastatingly rich soured cream. By early March there are few vegetables – carrots, potatoes and cabbage were about all we ever saw – and little fruit to be had. After a long snow-bound winter the islanders, the Lofot, are anticipating the coming of spring and a flush of new greenery to invigorate the diet. They are almost at the end of the store of golden cloudberries and dark blueberries, bottled or frozen during the previous summer.

It was Wenche who cooked us our first taste of the local cod. To say that it was boiled sounds distinctly drab and unpromising, but it was outstandingly good. This is partly to do with the method (see p.206), and even more with the unparalleled freshness which turns familiar old cod into a fish worthy of kings. Wenche introduced us to other cooks and notables around the islands. At Reine we met Hartvig Sverdrup, the local *vaereier*, fish lord of the village. To be fair, he wouldn't lay claim to the title, but for generations his family has owned the place lock, stock and barrel. His business is similar to that of the Statles, but run on a grander scale, that still bears traces of banished feudalism.

Way back on the road to Svolvaer, there's a turning off to one of Lofoten's largest and most picturesque ports. Henningsvaer juts out into the sea, barely changed, on the surface at least, in years with its painted wooden houses and quays. It was in Henningsvaer that we tasted one of Norway's most loved and cherished delicacies, a favourite for Christmas festivities. *Lutefisk*, I have to say, is an acquired taste and one that neither I nor William have mastered. Traditionally the man of a household was the one who undertook the lengthy preparation. Nowadays it is,

Hanging cod up to dry, Mortsund.

more often than not, bought ready-prepared from a specialist like Harold Bardewick. Let me explain the process. Stockfish, as hard as a bone, is soaked for 4–7 days in frequent changes of water. Next it is plunged into a lye solution – actually water spiked with a shot of caustic soda – and left for 2 days or longer, according to taste. The caustic soda, which is not a substance our bodies take to happily, must then be thoroughly washed out, which is done by submerging the *lutefisk* in running water for several more days. Then, and only then, is it ready to cook!

Merri Bardewick, Harold's wife, invited us to her home to sample *lutefisk* in its full glory, boiled and dressed with sizzling pork fat and bacon cubes. I liked the bacon and I liked the carrot stew that went with the main course. The Bardewick family are enchantingly warm and welcoming, and we had a great evening. But the *lutefisk* ... sorry, not my cup of tea. That bizarre jellyish consistency and terminal blandness seems a cruel destiny for what was once good fresh Lofoten cod.

Ⓥ

Neslesuppe
Nettle Soup

Admittedly this recipe was given to me by a Swedish woman who runs a restaurant in Ireland (the highly recommended Dunworley Cottage, County Cork), but nettle soup is made in the spring in Norway with much enthusiasm. Katherine Noren's recipe just happens to be one of the best I've come across.

You will, of course, need to arm yourself with a pair of sturdy rubber gloves for this soup. Suitably adorned, you should then hunt down a vigorous patch of nettles as far away from the roads as possible. In early spring the entire tender young nettle can be used. By May you should nip off only the nettle tops. Once summer sets in properly, the season is past and nettles are far too fibrous for culinary use. By the way, 8 oz (225 g) nettles is a fair amount. To be on the safe side, pick enough to fill two plastic carrier bags loosely.

Those of you who are not so inclined to go hunting for nettles could substitute 1 lb (450 g) spinach. Reduce the quantity of water by about half at first, adding more as needed, since spinach leaves tend to give up copious amounts of liquid as they cook.

SERVES 6

generous 8 oz (225 g) very young nettles or nettle tops (see above)	1 lb (450 g) onions, sliced
4 oz (100 g) butter	salt and pepper
4 cloves garlic, peeled	whipped cream to serve

Pick over the nettles and discard any damaged leaves. Wash well in several changes of water. Melt the butter in a large pan and add the whole cloves of garlic and the onions. Fry until tender and slightly browned. Add the nettles, 2 pints (1.2 litres) water, salt and pepper. Bring to the boil and simmer for 5 minutes or so, until tender. Liquidize, then return to the pan and bring back to the boil. Taste and adjust the seasoning. When serving, dollop a generous spoonful of whipped cream on each bowl of soup.

Henningsvaer Fiskesuppe
Henningsvaer Fish Soup

This is a scandalously rich and delicious fish soup. We ate it at Otto Åsheim's restaurant, Fiskekrogen, in Henningsvaer, then just had to go back a few days later for more. I was told that Otto would never give me the recipe, apparently a closely-guarded secret, but when it came down to it, he didn't bat an eyelid. It's really a version of the more southerly Bergen fish soup, and the real secret is the addition of vinegar and sugar, which cleverly cuts through the creaminess.

SERVES 6–8

12 oz (350 g) cod fillet
2 oz (50 g) butter
1 onion, finely chopped
1 large carrot, finely chopped
1 large leek (both white and green parts), finely chopped

2 teaspoons caster sugar
2 tablespoons white wine vinegar
salt and pepper
10 fl oz (300 ml) crème fraîche, or soured cream mixed with double cream
chopped fresh parsley

Fish stock

1 lb (450 g) bones and skin from white fish
1 carrot, sliced
1 large leek, quartered
1 stick celery, sliced

1 glass dry white wine
1 bay leaf
2 sprigs of fresh parsley
4 black peppercorns

First make the stock. Put all the ingredients in a large pan and add 3 pints (1.75 litres) of water. Bring to the boil and simmer for 20 minutes. Cool and strain.

Bring the stock to the boil. Add the cod, bring gently back to the boil and then draw off the heat. When tepid, lift out the cod and flake, discarding the skin and any stray bones. Reserve the flesh and stock.

Melt the butter in a large pan and add the vegetables. Stir to coat nicely in fat, then cover the pan, reduce the heat to very low and leave to sweat for 20 minutes, stirring once or twice. Add the stock, sugar, vinegar, salt and pepper and bring to the boil. Simmer for 10 minutes. Stir in the crème fraîche and the flaked fish. Taste and adjust the seasoning, then re-heat gently without boiling. Serve immediately, sprinkled with a little chopped parsley.

Gravlaks
Cured Salmon with Mustard and Dill Sauce

Before you protest, I know that Gravlaks, or Gravad Lax, is originally Swedish, but Norwegian salmon is of sterling quality and the Norwegians have quite justifiably annexed their neighbours' way of curing it. Some Norwegian recipes add a tot of brandy to the curing mixture, but I prefer the simpler blend of salt, sugar, pepper and dill.

Though we tend to serve it, rather like smoked salmon, as a first course with thin slices of buttered bread, the Norwegians go for a more robust and generous presentation. Thickly sliced, it may come with a plate of salad and hot boiled potatoes; or it can be fried in butter for a hot supper dish.

Alternatively, it might be grilled in portion-sized pieces, skin-side to the heat, without turning, for 8–10 minutes until the skin is crisply browned. By this time the flesh will be all but cooked through, still slightly translucent on the surface.

If you do prefer to stick with the thinly sliced, raw-cured salmon, don't waste the skin. Dry-fry it, or grill briefly until it crisps up, and serve it hot with the cold Gravlaks, or as a nibble with drinks.

S E R V E S 8 as a first course

2 lb (900 g) very fresh salmon fillet
1 tablespoon coarse sea salt
2 level tablespoons sugar

2 tablespoons finely chopped dill or
1 tablespoon dried dill
1 tablespoon black peppercorns, coarsely crushed

If you conveniently have 2 (or 4) portions of fillet all of roughly the same shape, leave them as they are. If you have 1 large piece or, say, 3 smaller ones, cut them so that they can be sandwiched together neatly.

Find a shallow dish that will take the pieces of salmon fillet sandwiched together in a snug layer. Mix all the remaining ingredients. Sprinkle 2 tablespoons of this mixture over the base of the dish and lay the first salmon pieces, skin-side down, on top. Spread most of the remaining mixture over the salmon and lay the second pieces, skin-side up, on top. Scatter over remaining seasoning mix. Cover with cling film or foil, weigh down with a board or plate and leave for 24 hours in the refrigerator, turning the salmon sandwich once or twice. It can be stored like this for up to 4 days in the refrigerator.

To serve, wipe the salmon clean and slice thinly, like smoked salmon. A very sharp knife is essential, and it helps to pop the salmon into the freezer for 10–15 minutes beforehand to firm it up. Accompany with the mustard and dill sauce below.

Ⓥ

Dill- og Sennepssaus
Mustard and Dill Sauce

Somewhere between a vinaigrette and a mayonnaise, with lots of mustard and dill and a little sugar to sweeten. You can leave out the raw egg yolk if you prefer, but the sauce won't be quite so thick and luscious.

SERVES 6–8

2 tablespoons Dijon mustard
1 egg yolk (optional, but a good addition)
1 level tablespoon caster sugar
5 fl oz (150 ml) sunflower or
    groundnut oil

1 tablespoon white wine vinegar
3 tablespoons chopped fresh dill
salt and pepper

Mix the mustard, egg yolk (if using) and sugar. Gradually whisk in the oil as if you were making a mayonnaise (though it's not quite such a temperamental process). Stir in vinegar, dill, salt and pepper. Taste and adjust the seasoning.

Torskekaviar
Fresh Cod Caviar

Norway's answer to taramasalata! *This is made all over the Lofoten Islands, both commercially and in homes. It is more usual to begin with a smoked roe (not the same as the heftily smoked ones we get here), but fresh cod's roe is a fine substitute. Some home cooks add a few drops of smoke essence (you can buy it here in specialist shops to flavour meat for barbecues), but to be honest I don't think it adds much to the finished 'caviar'.*

Either way, it is fairly strong stuff, and a little goes a long way. Serve the caviar on flat rye breads or hot toast, perhaps with a sprinkling of chopped onion, and a dab or two of soured cream for those who want it. Or turn it into a dip, as they do in Reine, by mixing caviar, cream, onion and a little parsley.

SERVES 8–12, depending
on size of roe

6 oz (175 g) coarse salt
3 oz (75 g) granulated or caster sugar
1 whole raw cod's roe
sunflower or olive oil

Mix the salt and sugar. Spread out about one-third of it in a bowl that will take the cod's roe fairly neatly and snugly. Lay the roe on the bed of salt/sugar and then cover with the remaining mixture, making sure that it is completely submerged (if necessary, mix together a little more salt and sugar in a 2:1 ratio). Leave in the refrigerator, turning once or twice, for 3 days. The salt and sugar will eventually dissolve into a brine. Take the roe out of the brine, wipe dry, then set on a rack and leave to dry in the refrigerator for 24 hours.

Halve each lobe lengthways and scrape out the eggs into a processor or mincer. Whizz in short bursts, gradually adding 2 fl oz (50 ml) water and then about 5 fl oz (150 ml) oil. By the time all that is in, the mixture should be creamy but still slightly knobbly. Taste – it should be fairly strongly flavoured, but if it seems too overwhelming, beat in more oil. Store in the refrigerator in an airtight container, covered by a thin layer of oil.

Pytt i Panne
Meat and Potato Hash

Waste not want not, particularly in a country where the shortage of grazing land makes meat a luxury. Pytt i Panne *is an admirable way of stretching the remains of yesterday's roast round today's hungry bellies. The bellies' owners should count themselves lucky, as the hash of meat and potato is a treat, particularly when lubricated with a shot of cream.*

It bears a considerable resemblance to American corned beef hash, and is usually served with a fried egg perched on top of each plateful.

SERVES 4

2 onions, chopped

2 oz (50 g) butter

4 rashers smoked back bacon, cut into strips

1½ lb (750 g) boiled potatoes, skinned and diced

about 8–12 oz (225–350 g) left-over cooked beef or other meat, diced

2 tablespoons chopped fresh parsley

salt and pepper

5 tablespoons single cream (optional but very nice!)

4 fried eggs to serve (optional)

Fry the onions in half the butter until golden. Scoop out of the pan and reserve. Add the remaining butter to the pan and fry the bacon and diced potato fairly briskly until they brown appetizingly. Now add the cooked meat, fried onions, the parsley, salt and pepper and stir until piping hot. If using cream, pour that over too and bring back to a simmer. Serve immediately, topped, if you like, with a fried egg per person.

OVERLEAF
Left: *Fiskekaker* with *Rekesaus* (Fish Cakes with Shrimp Sauce) see p.204.
Right: *Gravlaks* (Cured Salmon with Mustard and Dill Sauce) see p.196.

Fiskepudding, Fiskeboller eller Fiskekaker
Fish Pudding, Fish Balls or Fish Cakes

The same mixture (fiskefarse) is used to make the characteristically Norwegian fish pudding, or individual fish cakes (which I like best) or poached fish balls. In Norway these three are always virgin white, but, not being such a purist, I've added a little colour and extra flavour with a sprinkling of chopped parsley, which you should omit for authenticity. Balls, cakes or pudding all may be served with the shrimp sauce on p.204, or the egg and butter sauce on p.207.

Left-over fish pudding can be sliced and used as a filling in sandwiches, or re-heated quickly in butter.

S E R V E S 6−8

Basic fish mixture

2 lb (900 g) boned and skinned fresh haddock	3 tablespoons chopped fresh parsley (not traditional, but I like it!)
8 fl oz (250 ml) full-cream milk	salt
2 tablespoons cornflour	8 fl oz (250 ml) crème fraîche, or soured cream mixed with double cream
freshly grated nutmeg	

Cut the fish up roughly and process in 3 batches with just enough of the milk to smooth it out. Keep processing in several long bursts, scraping down the sides of the bowl every now and then, until the purée is very smooth. Scoop into a bowl to finish the mixing by hand – this apparently is where the skill comes into it, and cannot be replicated in a processor! Sprinkle over the cornflour, nutmeg, parsley and salt and mix evenly.

Mix the remaining milk with the crème fraîche, and slowly beat it into the fish mixture a little at a time until it is light and fluffy. The mixture can be used to make fish pudding, fish balls or fish cakes (the one that gets my vote) or as described below.

Fiskepudding
Fish Pudding

butter
fine dry breadcrumbs
1 quantity basic fish mixture (see above)

Pre-heat the oven to 325°F (160°C), gas mark 3.

Generously butter a 3-pint (1.75-litre) mould (a loaf tin seems to work best) and sprinkle with breadcrumbs. Turn and tip the mould so that it is evenly coated and shake out any excess. Spoon the fish mixture into the mould and smooth down lightly. Cover with buttered foil and tie securely with string. Stand in a deep ovenproof dish and pour in enough boiling water to come about half-way up the sides of the mould. Bake in the oven for about 1 hour. The water around the mould should do no more than barely simmer. If it threatens to boil, reduce the heat.

The pudding is done when it is firm to the touch, and when a skewer inserted into the centre comes out dry. Remove it from the oven, allow to stand for 5 minutes and loosen the sides gently with a knife. Cover with a warm serving dish, invert and give it a firm shake to loosen the pudding. Quite a lot of liquid will begin to seep out and should be carefully drained off. Lift off the mould to reveal the creamy-white fish pudding. Serve hot.

Fiskeboller
Fish Balls

---

1 quantity of basic fish mixture
   (see p.202)
milk
salt

Optional flavourings

---

1 bay leaf
1−2 slices onion
few sprigs of fresh parsley

Chill the fish mixture for 30 minutes in the refrigerator. Using 2 dessertspoons, make small rugby-ball-shaped croquettes of it. Chill again until needed. Pour enough milk into a shallow pan to give a depth of about 1−1½ inches (2.5−4 cm). If you wish, add a bay leaf, a slice or two of onion and a few sprigs of parsley for extra flavour. Heat until barely simmering and then turn the heat down low. Poach the fish balls in the milk for 5 minutes or so, until just firm, carefully turning once. Scoop out into a shallow serving dish. Season the milk with salt and spoon a little of it over to make a thin sauce. Alternatively serve with hot melted butter, shrimp sauce (see p.204) or egg and butter sauce (see p.207) or float in soup.

Fiskekaker
Fish Cakes

1 quantity basic fish mixture (see p.202)
butter, or butter and oil for frying

Chill the fish mixture for 30 minutes in the refrigerator. Shape generous tablespoons of it into small, flat, round cakes about ½ inch (1 cm) thick. Fry in butter or butter and oil until browned.

Rekesaus
Shrimp Sauce

SERVES 4–6

1 lb (450 g) cooked shrimps or small
    prawns in their shells
10 fl oz (300 ml) fish stock
1 oz (25 g) butter
1 oz (25 g) flour

5 fl oz (150 ml) double cream
generous squeeze of lemon juice
1 tablespoon finely chopped fresh dill
salt and pepper

Shell the shrimps or prawns. Process the shells and heads to a rough chop of debris and put into a pan with the fish stock. Bring to the boil and simmer for 10 minutes. Strain and reserve the stock. Chop the shrimps or prawns roughly.

Melt the butter and stir in the flour. Stir over a low heat for 1 minute, then draw off the heat. Gradually mix in the stock, a little at a time, to form a smooth sauce. Then stir in the cream. Bring back to the boil and simmer for 5 minutes. Stir in the shrimps or prawns and simmer for a further minute or so. Add a generous squeeze of lemon juice, the dill and salt and pepper to taste.

Fiskegrateng
Fish Gratin

Mmm, this is a wickedly creamy, luxurious sort of a gratin, the type one shouldn't eat too often, tempting though it is. The cream and egg yolks give the sauce a voluptuous texture, and the pungency of Parmesan sets it all off brilliantly. Shrimps or prawns may be optional, but I'd be loath to leave them out.

SERVES 4 generously

1½ lb (750 g) white fish fillets (such as cod or haddock)
salt and pepper
1 tablespoon lemon juice
1½ oz (45 g) butter
1 oz (25 g) flour
10 fl oz (300 ml) milk
5 fl oz (150 ml) single cream

4 oz (100 g) cooked shrimps or prawns (shelled weight), roughly chopped (optional)
2 egg yolks
2 oz (50 g) Parmesan or other full-flavoured hard cheese, freshly grated

Pre-heat the oven to 350°F (180°C), gas mark 4.

Put the fish fillets into a lightly buttered ovenproof dish and season with salt, pepper and lemon juice. Cover with foil and bake in the oven for about 20 minutes, until just cooked. Drain off any liquid and quickly flake fish, discarding the skin. Place in a shallow gratin dish.

Meanwhile melt 1½ oz (45 g) of the butter in a saucepan and stir in the flour. Stir for a minute, then draw off the heat and gradually mix in the milk, a little at a time, followed by the cream. Simmer for 5–10 minutes, until thick, with no trace of raw flour taste. Draw off the heat again and stir in the shrimps or prawns (if using), then the egg yolks, salt and pepper. Pour over the cooked fish and sprinkle with Parmesan. Whip under a pre-heated grill until nicely browned.

If you've cooked the fish in advance, or are using left-overs from another meal, prepare as above, but finish the gratin in the oven at about 375°F (190°C), gas mark 5, baking until nicely browned – about 20–25 minutes.

Kokt Skrei med Leversaus
Boiled Cod with Liver Sauce

Torsk *is the usual word for cod, but everyone on Lofoten knows that the best cod is the* skrei *that arrives to spawn in late winter, heavy with roe. It is usually served with a buttery-tasting sauce made from the liver.*

We may have to make do with plain torsk *here, and without the liver sauce (though cod's roe is available at least during the winter months from good fishmongers), but even the most ordinary of cod is improved beyond measure by the Norwegian method of boiling fish. In the absence of liver, serve it with the egg and butter sauce on p.207 and a few boiled potatoes.*

S E R V E S 4

1 raw cod's roe
4 very fresh cod steaks, cut about ¾ inch
    (2 cm) thick
salt
4 tablespoons white wine vinegar

Cod Liver Sauce

1 cod liver
1 bay leaf
1 tablespoon white wine vinegar

Start by preparing the cod liver if you have it. Put it into a bowl of water and pull it apart with your fingers, discarding the membranes. Tear the liver up into small pieces, then drain. When you are ready to make the sauce, bring about 10 fl oz (300 ml) water to the boil with the bay leaf. Add the vinegar and liver and bring back to the boil. Add another 5 fl oz (150 ml) cold water and again bring back to the boil. That's it.

For the cod itself, fill a saucepan large enough to take the roe and steaks with enough water to come about two-thirds of the way up the sides. Add lots of salt, stirring to dissolve. The water should be as salty as sea-water. Wrap the roe in greaseproof paper and place it in the pan. Bring to the boil and simmer for about 10–15 minutes, until the roe is just firm. Add the vinegar and then the cod steaks. Bring slowly back to the boil, let it bubble for 1 minute, then turn off the heat, cover and allow to stand for 5 minutes or so, until the cod is cooked through.

Serve the cod with the liver sauce (re-heated if necessary) or egg and butter sauce (see p.207).

Ⓥ
Egg- og Smørsaus
Egg and Butter Sauce

This sauce comes as a welcome accompaniment to any plainly cooked fish, or to the fish pudding on p.202. A splash of vinegar can be added to sharpen it slightly if you wish. For a horseradish sauce, replace the eggs with a spoonful of freshly grated horseradish.

SERVES 4

4–6 oz (100–175 g) butter
2 hard-boiled eggs, shelled and chopped
2 tablespoons chopped fresh parsley
    (optional)
splash of white wine vinegar (optional)

Melt the butter, without letting it boil. Stir in the eggs, and the parsley and vinegar if using.

Ⓥ
Gulrotstuing
Carrot Stew

A side-dish rather than a centre-fold stew, this makes a pleasing change from everyday boiled carrots.

SERVES 4

1 lb (450 g) carrots, peeled and thickly
    sliced
dash of cider vinegar
salt and pepper

2 oz (50 g) butter
2 oz (50 g) flour
10 fl oz (300 ml) milk
freshly grated nutmeg

Put the carrots in a pan with the vinegar, salt and enough water to cover. Bring to the boil and simmer until tender. Drain, reserving the cooking water. Mash the carrots coarsely.

Melt the butter in a separate pan and sprinkle over the flour. Stir to make a *roux* and cook for 1 minute. Gradually stir in about 5 fl oz (150 ml) of the carrot cooking water to form a smooth paste, then stir in the milk to make a thick sauce. Simmer for 5 minutes, then add the carrots and plenty of freshly grated nutmeg. Warm through for a further minute or so, then taste and adjust the seasoning.

ⓥ
Rømmegrøt
Sour-cream Porridge

Rømmegrøt is not a porridge at all, but for some reason that is how it always gets described in English, probably because there's precious little else to compare it with. It is a curious sort of a pudding, much beloved in Norway, a little odd to foreign palates, but definitely worth trying.

We ate this at the Bardewicks', after the fascinatingly unappealing lutefisk. *They, like many other Norwegians, eat it with salami and dried cured lamb, as well as sugar! We Brits limited ourselves, in a disappointingly conservative way, to cinnamon and sugar.*

Don't even think of trying to make it with ordinary soured cream. For the pudding to succeed, you need the high butterfat content of crème fraîche, the nearest substitute there is for Norwegian soured cream.

SERVES 6–8

1 pint (600 ml) crème fraîche
3 pints (1.75 litres) milk
6 oz (175 g) plain flour
sugar and cinnamon to serve

Put the crème fraîche into a large pan set over a gentle heat. Stir until smooth and simmer gently, covered, for 10 minutes. Meanwhile set the milk to heat gently in a separate pan. After 10 minutes, sift about one-third of the flour into the crème fraîche, stirring constantly. Continue beating until smooth and the butterfat begins to separate out (you'll see this happening very clearly). Skim the butterfat off with a little ladle or spoon and collect in a small jug. Continue skimming the butterfat as it separates, stirring the cream occasionally to prevent it catching on the base of the pan, until you have collected 2½–3 fl oz (65–85 ml).

Now gradually beat about half the warm milk into the crème fraîche mixture, slowly at first, to give a smooth sauce. Sift in the remaining flour, stirring constantly, and, when it is fully incorporated, stir in the remaining milk. Keep stirring and heating through for a further 5 minutes or so, until piping hot.

Ladle into shallow bowls and pour a puddle of the reserved butterfat into the centre of each dish. Sprinkle with sugar and cinnamon and serve, with extra sugar and cinnamon handed around separately for those who want it.

Ⓥ
Brødpudding med Epler
Bread Pudding with Apples

I can't truthfully claim that this is something we tucked into while we were in the Lofoten Islands. If I'm honest, I must admit that it's a recipe I came across, and took a fancy to, in James and Elizabeth White's Good Food from Denmark and Norway *(Frederick Muller Ltd), published back in 1959, the year I was born! I love bread pudding, and the addition of tart apple purée made this version irresistible.*

SERVES 4–6

12 oz (350 g) cooking apples
finely grated zest of ½ lemon
4 oz (100 g) caster sugar
8 thin slices of bread
softened butter

2 oz (50 g) flaked almonds
10 fl oz (300 ml) milk
5 fl oz (150 ml) double cream
2 eggs

Peel and core the apples and cut roughly into chunks. Put into a pan with 2 tablespoons water and the lemon zest, cover and stew over a low heat until the juices begin to run. Raise the heat and cook until the apples have collapsed to a thick purée. Sweeten to taste.

Butter the slices of bread on both sides. Spread with apple purée, quarter, and layer in a baking dish, scattering almonds between the layers. Beat the milk with the cream, about 2 oz (50 g) sugar and the eggs. Pour over the bread and leave for 1 hour, so that the bread can soak up the milk.

Pre-heat the oven to 325°F (160°C), gas mark 3. Stand the dish in a roasting tin and pour boiling water around it to a depth of about 1 inch (2.5 cm). Bake in the oven for 30–40 minutes, until just set. Serve hot.

Notes on Using
the Recipes

- Always stick with following either the metric or imperial measurements for the ingredients, never a mixture of the two.

- All spoon measurements are rounded, unless otherwise stated.

- All eggs are size 2.

- I always use extra virgin olive oil for cooking, but if you prefer a milder flavour then stay with plain olive oil.

Ⓥ

Vegetarian Symbol

The Ⓥ sign denotes recipes that are suitable for vegetarians but please note that some recipes include dairy products.

Alternative Ingredients

Air-dried beef See *Bündnerfleisch*.

Air-dried ham/*prosciutto*/*jamón serrano* Italy, Spain, Portugal and even the UK all produce air-dried hams, some of them smoked. The most famous is Parma ham, an Italian *prosciutto*, but Spanish *jamón serrano*, particularly the hams from Jabugo, are every bit as good. The Portuguese version is called *presunto*. Any of these may be used in cooking, but since the top-rank air-dried hams are all extremely expensive, it makes sense to use, say, an anonymous *prosciutto* rather than a named premium-priced Parma or San Daniele. Delicatessens will often sell offcuts quite cheaply, or may let you have the bone, once the ham has all been carved, for flavouring soups and stocks. Though these hams of different nationalities all have differing characteristics, they can be used interchangeably in recipes.

Alpkäse This Swiss term simply means a cheese that has been made high up in the alp, as opposed to *Bergkäse*, made lower down in the village. There are many different types of *Alpkäse*. Most of the ones we tasted in the Graubunden were fairly mild, with a rubbery but soft texture. The Lerchis' own *Alpkäse* was particularly good – very rich and buttery. Taste depends too on the maturity of the cheese. In most of the Swiss recipes I've substituted Gruyère, which is sweeter but works well.

Anchovy fillets Where anchovy fillets are included among the ingredients in a recipe, I've usually assumed that you will be using tinned anchovy fillets, in olive oil.

However, most of the anchovies used around the Mediterranean will have been preserved in salt rather than oil. If you have a Greek, Italian or Spanish delicatessen near you, you may find that they stock salted anchovies (and sardines). These are delicious, but need special treatment. For a start, they usually come whole, so fillet them first. Soak the fillets in milk for at least 30 minutes to draw out some of the salt. Then they are ready to use. If you have some prepared fillets left over, preserve them in olive oil in an airtight jar.

Armagnac One of the most famous types of brandy, made in Gascony, where it is, naturally, considered infinitely superior to any other – in particular Cognac, its avowed rival It does have an intensely vivid, powerful flavour and aroma, both of which are employed to great effect in cooking. If you can't get Armagnac, or quite justifiably prefer to keep it for drinking, substitute a lesser French brandy.

Baccalà/bacalao/bacalhau See salt cod.

Bündnerfleisch Air-dried beef from the Graubünden in Switzerland. It is cured and served in thin slices like an air-dried ham. As a substitute, air-dried ham isn't bad going, though of course the flavour is not a perfect match.

Ceps/Penny Buns/*Boletus edulis* Large, meaty, wild mushrooms (*cèpes* in French), found all over Europe and very highly prized. Even if you never learn to identify any other wild mushroom, at least find out what the *Boletus edulis* looks like. It's far too good to miss, and they don't come cheap if you have to buy them.

All types of *Boletus* mushrooms are distinguished by their sponge-like gills, and this one is quite distinctive. All but two types of *Boletus* are edible, and the two exceptions are easy to spot. Always check identification two or three times with a good reference book, to make 100 per cent sure that you have exactly the mushroom you think you have, and then double-check that it isn't either of the toxic ones.

Chanterelles Another type of wild mushroom, almost as good as ceps. The chanterelle, though, is smaller, orange-yellow and funnel-shaped. Unless you go mushrooming with an expert, it's probably best to resist woodland temptation (they are not so easy to identify as ceps), and to limit yourself to the occasional splurge when you see them for sale. Do check that you are buying prime quality. There's nothing more dispiriting than getting home and discovering that half your gold-dust mushrooms are soggy and old and going mouldy. The odd bit of worm-damage is just nature, but avoid those that are so riddled with holes that there's precious little left for humans.

Chorizo/*chouriço* Spanish *chorizo* is a delicious type of cured pork sausage flavoured with paprika. It can be either mild (*dulce*) or hot and spicy (*picante*). There's another choice to be made too. Some *chorizo* is dried fairly hard, like a salami, ideal served thinly sliced as part of an hors d'oeuvre, though it can also be used as a flavouring in cooking. Ideally what you want for cooking is the softer sort of *chorizo*, semi-dried, usually not much more than 1 inch (2.5 cm) in diameter. This is what I mean when I've listed 'cooking *chorizo*' among the ingredients for a recipe.

Good Italian delicatessens will usually stock all kinds of *chorizo*. Don't be tempted to buy what is sometimes described as 'Spanish-style *chorizo*', often sold in supermarkets, and made outside Spain or Portugal. It's disgusting. Real *chorizo* has a bright paprika-red colour – don't be conned into buying anything less.

Portuguese *chouriço* is similar to but not quite the same as Spanish *chorizo*. It tends to be fattier, with its own blend of spicing, though paprika remains predominant. It's hard to find here, so you'll probably have to settle for the Spanish kind.

Crème fraîche See soured cream.

***Croustade* pastry** See filo pastry.

Eau-de-vie de prunes French plum 'brandy'. This is a strong, clear, unsweetened spirit with a heady flavour of plums. It is widely used around Agen, plum-capital of France.

Filo pastry/*Strudel* pastry/*croustade* pastry Though purists would no doubt argue the differences between these three until the cows come home, in practice filo pastry functions well in place of both *Strudel* and *croustade* dough. Besides, unless you make your own – and that's a skilled job – you're unlikely to be able to obtain anything here but filo pastry. It's worth trying different brands as some are much thinner than others, and maximum thinness is the essential quality for all of these pastries.

Dimensions vary considerably from one manufacturer to another. Where it matters, I've indicated the size I used, but usually it is easy enough to adapt to whatever you've got.

Hamburg parsley See parsley root.

Jamón serrano See air-dried ham.

Kaymak This stuff is so over-the-top and luxurious; it is clotted sheep's milk cream, served in Turkey with many of their syrup-soaked pastries. It is so thick that it can be sliced, or shaped into curls like butter. The nearest thing here is clotted cream.

Morcilla Spanish blood sausage (there's a Portuguese equivalent, too, called *morcelas*), spicier than our own, and often with more fat, or softened with rice. If you can't get *morcilla*, substitute a good British black pudding or French *boudin noir*.

Olive oil I always use extra-virgin olive oil for all cooking purposes, diluting it occasionally with sunflower or groundnut oil where I want a milder flavour, or when deep-frying. Extra-virgin olive oil has a more powerful flavour than the stuff that is sold as plain olive oil (which has been highly processed), though this varies from one brand to another and from one country to another. It's really a question of experimentation, to find something that you like. Since a wide range of olive oils of all sorts is now readily available, that shouldn't present too much of a problem.

Pancetta Italian 'bacon', though that is a slight misnomer. *Pancetta* is very fatty, and has a particular flavour that marks it out. It is always used as a flavouring (not really suitable for a bacon butty, for instance). *Pancetta affumicata* has been smoked. Buy *pancetta* from Italian delicatessens, but if you really can't lay your hands on any, ordinary streaky bacon is a tolerable substitute.

Paprika Merely dried, finely ground, mild, red peppers (as in capsicums rather than peppercorns). However, that is by no means the end of the story. Spanish paprika, which is mildly smoky, is markedly different from the Hungarian variety, with more of a metallic tinge: not surprising, as they are ground from different cultivars. Unfortunately most of the paprika sold in this country is anonymous, and we just have to use whatever we can get. Spanish delicatessens may stock proper Spanish paprika or *pimentón*, and if you are extremely lucky you may come across real Hungarian paprika in eastern European delis – worth looking for.

Parma ham See air-dried ham.

Parmesan cheese Never, ever buy it ready grated in little tubs. That's vile stuff, stale and old and stinky. Parmesan should always be bought in a piece and grated when needed. You'll be amazed by the difference. Store hunks of Parmesan wrapped in foil in the refrigerator, but open them up once every couple of days for a quick breath of fresh air. If you have a huge amount, perhaps carried back from an Italian holiday, wrap it tightly and freeze. It can be grated straight from the frozen block.

Parsley root/Hamburg parsley This is exactly what it sounds like – the root of a type of parsley. It looks similar to a parsnip, a little whiter perhaps, and has a distinct parsley taste. I have occasionally come across parsley root in shops selling organic vegetables, but it is a rare find. The nearest substitute is celeriac, at least in texture and degree of sweetness, if not in precise flavour.

Ricotta cheese Buy fresh ricotta from a good Italian delicatessen if at all possible, and use it up within 24 hours before it develops a bitter after-taste. Supermarket tubs and vacuum-packs of ricotta don't rate that highly, though if all else fails they will do. Sicilian ricotta is often mildly salted, unlike ricotta from the mainland. It is also much softer and creamier than any sort of ricotta I've found here, so much so that when sieved it can be beaten to a cream with no additions. Where necessary, I've added a few tablespoons of milk to the recipes to achieve the same effect.

Salt cod/*baccalà* (Italy)/*bacalao* (Spain)/*bacalhau* (Portugal) William has written at length on salt cod in the chapter on Portugal, so I'm sticking to basics. Portuguese, Spanish and Italian delicatessens may all sell salt cod, cutting it from a whole triangular side. Try to get as much of the fatter central part as possible, rather than the thinner edges. If you draw a blank on the deli front, you could try looking in West Indian foodshops, where salt cod is often sold cut up and pre-wrapped in small packages. The quality tends not to be quite so good, and of course you can't check that you're getting a fair share of the thicker section.

To prepare salt cod, soak it for at least 24 hours in plenty of cold water, changing the water a minimum of three times during that period, more often if possible. Some cod is so salty that it will need 36 hours' (or, more rarely, 48 hours') soaking, so be prepared. Taste a shred or two of the soaked cod to see how it is doing.

To cook, place in a shallow pan with enough water or milk, or a mixture of the two, just to cover. If you wish, add slices of onion, a few bay leaves and a sprig or two of parsley and bring gently to the boil. Poach until the fish flakes easily – around 8–15 minutes.

In most salt cod dishes, the fish is then cooked again with other ingredients, so take great care not to add more salt (it's very easy to do it automatically without thinking) until you've tasted the finished dish and are sure that it really needs it.

Soured cream/crème fraîche Continental soured creams are not the same as the soured cream sold here. They are almost invariably much, much richer, containing a higher percentage of butterfat. Our soured cream cannot be directly substituted in cooking as it is more than likely to curdle in a most unpleasant and unsightly manner.

Instead look out for French crème fraîche, which is becoming more and more widely available in supermarkets as well as in specialist shops. This has a greater butterfat content than even double cream and is perfect for sauces.

Your other option is to mix British soured cream with an equal quantity of double cream. Admittedly this softens the sourness, but it does boost the fat content. The blend can be used immediately, though the flavour will improve if it is left at room temperature for a few hours to mature.

Speck This is a type of bacon from Germany, often smoked and usually very fatty. It is fairly easy to buy here from delicatessen counters and is the nearest thing to the cured bacons used in both Switzerland and Hungary. It can usually be bought in a slab rather than ready-sliced, which is a bonus.

***Strudel* pastry** See filo pastry.

Sumac A marvellous Turkish and Middle Eastern spice, with a sourish taste and a beautiful, crystalline, dark red colour. It is usually sprinkled over fully prepared food – on salads, yoghurty dips or grilled meats and *köfte*. There's no adequate substitute, but you can manage without or make do with a squeeze of lemon juice.

Túró Hungarian curd cheese, fairly rich, something like a cross between ricotta and our own curd cheese, either of which make a passable substitute. A blend of the two would be ideal.

Vanilla sugar You can buy this in sachets, but you might just as well make your own. Stuff one or two whole vanilla pods into a jar of sugar. Close tightly and leave for a week or so before using. As the sugar level drops, just top up with more sugar. The vanilla pods can be used to scent custards or whatever, then rinsed, dried and popped back into the jar.

Wax peppers Medium-large, cone-shaped, pale green peppers with a mild flavour, widely grown and used in Hungary. They are sometimes sold here, but green peppers are fine as an alternative.

Recipe List

Main Courses: Poultry and Game
Arroz con conejo Rice with Rabbit (SPAIN) p.22
Palombes palombières Wood Pigeon Hunter-style (FRANCE) p.63
Lapin aux pruneaux d'Agen Rabbit with Prunes (FRANCE) p.64
Magret e canard au confit d'oignons Grilled Duck Breast with Caramelized Onion (FRANCE)
   p.65
Confit de canard Duck *Confit* (FRANCE) p.68
La poule-au-pot de Mme Fouteau Mme Fouteau's Chicken in a Pot (FRANCE) p.70
The Taxi-Driver's Coniglio a cacciatora Hunter's Rabbit (SICILY) p.104
Paprikás csirke Chicken Paprikash (HUNGARY) p.146

Main Courses: Vegetable, Pasta and Noodle dishes
Patatas a la extremeña Potato and Pepper Stew (SPAIN) p.25
Pasta con le melanzane Pasta with Fried Aubergine (ITALY) p.94
Pesto ericinese Basil, Almond and Tomato Pesto (ITALY) p.95
Tagliatelle con fave e pancetta Tagliatelle with Broad Beans and Pancetta (ITALY) p.96
Härdöpfelpitta Potato and Dried Pear Pancake Squares (SWITZERLAND) p.169
Maluns Fried Potato Crumbs with Apple Compote (SWITZERLAND) p.170
Käsesuppe Bread and Cheese Pudding (SWITZERLAND) p.171
Pizokels/Bizochels Dumpling Noodles (SWITZERLAND) p.172
Härdöpfel-Pizokels Pizokels with Potatoes and Speck (SWITZERLAND) p.173
Pizokels mit Spinat und Tomaten Pizokels with Spinach and Tomato (SWITZERLAND) p.173
Capuns Chard Parcels (SWITZERLAND) p.174

Salads
Salade aux endives et aux noix Chicory and Walnut Salad (FRANCE) p.74
Wurstsalat Sausage Salad (SWITZERLAND) p.178

Vegetable and Side Dishes
Cèpes à la grille Grilled Ceps (FRANCE) p.72
Cèpes à la persillade Ceps with Garlic and Parsley (FRANCE) p.73
Hünkar begendi Sultan's Delight (TURKEY) p.125
Galuska Little Egg Dumplings (HUNGARY) p.147
Lecso Green Pepper and Tomato Stew (HUNGARY) p.153
Vegyes téli savanyúság Mixed Salad Pickles (HUNGARY) p.154
Gulrotstuing Carrot Stew (NORWAY) p.207

Sauces
Salsa di pomodoro Tomato Sauce (ITALY) p.89
Tarator Garlic and Walnut Sauce (TURKEY) p.121
Sarımsaklı Yogurt Yoghurt and Garlic Sauce (TURKEY) p.131
Rekesaus Shrimp Sauce (NORWAY) p.204
Egg- og smørsaus Egg and Butter Sauce (NORWAY) p.207

Desserts

Tocino de cielo Heavenly Bacon (SPAIN) p.28
Repapalos Sweet Bread Dumplings (SPAIN) p.29
Leche frite Fried Custard (SPAIN) p.30
Pudim Molotov Light-as-air Pudding (PORTUGAL) p.50
Ovos moles Syrup Custard (PORTUGAL) p.51
Fatias reais Sweet Egg Bread in Syrup (PORTUGAL) p.52
Arroz doce Portuguese Rice Pudding (PORTUGAL) p.52
Pêssegos Herdade de Zambujal Baked Peaches in Wine (PORTUGAL) p.53
Pastéis de nata Custard Tarts (PORTUGAL) p.54
Glace à l'Armagnac et aux pruneaux Prune and Armagnac Ice-Cream (FRANCE) p.75
Croustade aux pommes Apple and Armagnac Filo Tart (FRANCE) p.76
Croustade aux pruneaux et aux pommes Apple and Prune Pie (FRANCE) p.78
Sorbetto di fragola Strawberry Sorbet (ITALY) p.105
Granita di fragola Strawberry Granita (ITALY) p.105
Biancomangiare Blancmange (ITALY) p.106
Cassatedde di ricotta Ricotta and Chocolate Fritters (ITALY) p.106
Torta di mandorle e ricotta Almond, Ricotta and Honey Cheesecake (ITALY) p.108
Baklava Syrup and Nut Pastry (TURKEY) p.132
İrmik helvacs Semolina Pudding (TURKEY) p.133
Revani Lemon Syrup Cake (TURKEY) p.134
Ayva tatlısı Quince Pudding (TURKEY) p.135
Mákos Patkó Beigli Poppy-seed Rolls (HUNGARY) p.155
Túrós lepény Baked Cheesecake (HUNGARY) p.158
Vera szilváslepénye Vera's Plum Tart (HUNGARY) p.159
Palacsinta Pancakes (HUNGARY) p.160
Palacsinta Gundel módra Gundel-style pancakes (HUNGARY) p.161
Linzertorte Raspberry and Almond Tart (SWITZERLAND) p.179
Engadiner Nusstorte Caramel Nut Tart (SWITZERLAND) p.180
Flambierte Zwetschgen in Butter überbacken Flambéed Buttered Plums (SWITZERLAND) p.181
Apfelstrudel Apple Strudel (SWITZERLAND) p.182
Rømmegrøt Sour-cream Porridge (NORWAY) p.208
Brødpudding med epler Bread Pudding with Apples (NORWAY) p.209

Bread and Biscuits

Simit Sesame Bread Rings (Turkish Bagels) (TURKEY) p.136
Burebrot Farmer's Bread (SWITZERLAND) p.183
Zopf Rich White Bread Plaits (SWITZERLAND) p.184
Birnbrot Dried Pear Bread (SWITZERLAND) p.186

Sundries

Confiture de figues Fig Jam (FRANCE) p.79
Gelée de coings Quince Jelly (FRANCE) p.80
Körözött juhturó Liptó Cheese Spread (HUNGARY) p.145
Bircher muesli Fresh Muesli (SWITZERLAND) p.188

Index

Numerals in *italics* indicate an illustration.